"This book represents a new maturity in spiritual thinking and teaching. David Benner is wise, broad and deep all at the same time. And you will be too after you finish this wonderful book."

Richard Rohr, O.F.M., Center for Action and Contemplation, Albuquerque, New Mexico

"In *Opening to God*, David Benner has given us a generous, comprehensive and very pastoral guide not only to the myriad types of prayer open to us as Christians, but also to the informing attitudes and physical nuances which can enable a rich prayer life in all of us."

Phyllis Tickle, compiler, *The Divine Hours*

"David Benner's *Opening to God* should become a classic! It is warm, wise, gentle and challenging. For the beginner or the experienced it offers guidance in the Christian prayer practice of *lectio divina,* making this ancient monastic approach to prayer wonderfully accessible to the contemporary seeker. By no means is it a rigid or opaque 'how to' book, but rather an invitation to go ever deeper in the life of prayer. Reading it is like a conversation with a trusted friend."

Margaret Guenther, Episcopal priest and author of
Holy Listening: The Art of Spiritual Direction and The Practice of Prayer

"*Opening to God* is an invitation to prayer—not just a book about prayer, but a guide for daily practice. Like an intimate retreat with a spiritual master, it brings centuries of wisdom close enough to speak to our lives. I've never met David Benner, but I felt like I was reading someone who'd listened to my prayers."

Jonathan Wilson-Hartgrove (jonathanwilsonhartgrove.com),
coauthor, *Becoming the Answer to Our Prayers*

"In *Opening to God*, David Benner has gifted us with a thoughtful and comprehensive guide to Christian prayer. The intimacy with which Benner writes about prayer betrays a deep and abiding knowledge of the subject, thus this book is destined to be valued by individuals and groups alike in their quest for more intimacy with God."

Tony Jones (tonyj.net), author of *The Sacred Way:
Spiritual Practices in Everyday Life*

Books by David G. Benner

Soulful Spirituality: Becoming Fully Alive and Deeply Human (Brazos Press, in
   press)

Opening to God: Lectio Divina and Life as Prayer (InterVarsity Press, 2010)

Desiring God's Will: Aligning Our Hearts with the Heart of God (InterVarsity
   Press, 2005)

The Gift of Being Yourself: The Sacred Call to Self-Discovery (InterVarsity Press,
   2004)

*Spiritual Direction and the Care of Souls: A Guide to Christian Approaches and
   Practices,* ed. with Gary Moon (InterVarsity Press, 2004)

Surrender to Love: Discovering the Heart of Christian Spirituality (InterVarsity
   Press, 2003)

Strategic Pastoral Counseling, 2nd ed. (Baker, 2003)

Sacred Companions: The Gift of Spiritual Friendship and Direction (InterVarsity
   Press, 2002)

Baker Encyclopedia of Psychology and Counseling, ed. with Peter Hill (Baker, 1999)

Free at Last: Breaking the Bondage of Guilt and Emotional Wounds (Essence,
   1999)

Care of Souls: Revisioning Christian Nurture and Counsel (Baker, 1998)

*Money Madness and Financial Freedom: The Psychology of Money Meanings and
   Management* (Detselig, 1996)

Choosing the Gift of Forgiveness, with Robert Harvey (Baker, 1996)

Understanding and Facilitating Forgiveness, with Robert Harvey (Baker, 1996)

Strategic Pastoral Counseling: A Short-Term Structured Model (Baker, 1992)

Christian Perspectives on Human Development, ed. with LeRoy Aden and
   J. Harold Ellens (Baker, 1992)

Counselling as a Spiritual Process (Clinical Theology Association, 1991)

Healing Emotional Wounds (Baker, 1990)

Counselling and the Human Predicament, ed. with LeRoy Aden (Baker, 1989)

Psychotherapy and the Spiritual Quest (Baker, 1988)

Psychology and Religion, ed. (Baker, 1987)

Psychotherapy in Christian Perspective, ed. (Baker, 1987)

Christian Counseling and Psychotherapy, ed. (Baker, 1987)

Therapeutic Love: An Incarnational Interpretation of Counselling (Clinical
   Theology Association, 1985)

Baker Encyclopedia of Psychology, ed. (Baker, 1985)

OPENING
TO GOD

LECTIO DIVINA AND LIFE AS PRAYER

DAVID G. BENNER

IVP Books

An imprint of InterVarsity Press
Downers Grove, Illinois

InterVarsity Press
P.O. Box 1400, Downers Grove, IL 60515-1426
World Wide Web: www.ivpress.com
E-mail: email@ivpress.com

InterVarsity Press® is the book-publishing division of InterVarsity Christian Fellowship/USA®, a
movement of students and faculty active on campus at hundreds of universities, colleges and schools
of nursing in the United States of America, and a member movement of the International Fellowship
of Evangelical Students. For information about local and regional activities, write Public Relations
Dept., InterVarsity Christian Fellowship/USA, 6400 Schroeder Rd., P.O. Box 7895, Madison, WI
53707-7895, or visit the IVCF website at <www.intervarsity.org>.

All Scripture quotations, unless otherwise indicated, are taken from The New Jerusalem Bible,
copyright 1985 by Darton, Longman & Todd, Ltd. and Doubleday, a division of Random House, Inc.
All rights reserved.

Design: Cindy Kiple
Images: Magda Indigo/Getty Images

ISBN 978-0-8308-3542-3

Printed in the United States of America ∞

Library of Congress Cataloging-in-Publication Data

Benner, David G.
  Opening to God: lectio divina and life as prayer / David G.
Benner.
    p. cm.
  Includes bibliographical references.
  ISBN 978-0-8308-3542-3 (cloth: alk. paper)
  1. Bible—Devotional use. 2. Prayer—Christianity. 3. Spiritual
life—Christianity. I. Title.
  BS617.8.B46 2010
  248.3'2—dc22

                                          2010014326

P	18	17	16	15	14	13	12	11	10	9	8	7	6	5	4	3	2	1
Y	24	23	22	21	20	19	18	17	16	15	14	13	12	11	10			

To my father

Gordon Wilson Benner

(1920-2007)

whose life was a prayer

and for whom prayer was his life

And to my friend

Fr. M. Basil Pennington, O.C.S.O.

(1931-2005)

who helped me discover *lectio divina*

as a framework for prayer and life

CONTENTS

ACKNOWLEDGMENTS

This book began as a series of talks at Christ Church Cathedral in Victoria, British Columbia, Canada, during Lent 2009. I wish to thank the Very Reverend Dr. Logan McMenamie, dean of Columbia and rector of the Cathedral, for inviting my wife and myself to deliver this series of Lenten meditations on prayer— her part also resulting in a book.[1] I also wish to thank those from the parish and community who attended these sessions and so helpfully interacted with me around the ideas I was trying to articulate.

I would also like to thank my agent, Kathy Helmers, for her assistance in the early stages of manuscript preparation, and my editor, Al Hsu, for his characteristically extremely helpful suggestions in the editing process. And, once again, I am happy to be able to acknowledge and thank my wife, Juliet, for her continuing role in my spiritual journey, particularly for the way she has modeled a life that is prayer. The opportunity to work with her in lecture, workshop and retreat contexts over the past several decades remains one of my life's most fulfilling experiences.

Thanks be to God!

INTRODUCTION

TRANSFORMING OPENNESS TO GOD

JUST IMAGINE HOW DIFFERENT YOUR LIFE would be if moment by moment you were constantly open to God. Think of how much your experience of yourself, others and the world would change if you were continuously attuned to the loving presence of God and allowed the life of God to flow into and through you with each breath. Such a life would itself be prayer, for, as we shall see, prayer is not simply words that we offer when we speak to God but an opening of our self to God.

Most of us live most of our lives somewhere between the extremes of being completely closed to God and completely open. This is why I speak of *opening*. Opening implies not just a position but a direction—a direction of movement toward full openness. It recognizes that, even for those of us who long to know deep communion and union with God, we are ambivalent about the vulnerability of the surrender that this involves. We are hesitant in our openness—often taking a tentative step toward it and then quickly pulling back again. Obstacles obstruct the channels of self that we long to open fully to God, blocking our capacity to receive the fullness of God's life. These obstacles can take many forms—psychological (i.e., our fears and unhealed wounds), theological (i.e., our distorted views of God) and spiritual (i.e., rigidly hanging onto spiritual practices that no longer bring us life). It is these sorts of blocks to openness that God longs to remove so that we can become increasingly open to God and full of the very life of God.

This is why prayer holds the possibility of being so transformational. Of course, through prayer God can touch the world. But first and foremost, through prayer God touches and changes us. We become whole as we learn to live in openness before God. And as we respond to God's constantly inflowing life, God touches the world.

The possibility of transformation lies right at the heart of Christian faith. Think of the promise of being born again or, if this term sounds too archaic or feels like a better fit with some other faith tradition than your own, of conversion or spiritual awakening. The magnitude of the changes implied in these concepts might be somewhat embarrassing to us when we feel discouraged by the extremely limited progress typically resulting from our spiritual self-improvement projects. But they do remind us that Christianity is built on a hope that in Christ all will be made new.

Transformation is foundational to spirituality. Unlike religiosity, which can involve nothing more than beliefs and practices, spirituality involves a journey. Much more than a mere identity, it is walking a path. This is, of course, particularly clear in the case of Christian spirituality since the earliest followers of Jesus were called people of the Way. And prayer has been central to that Way since Jesus was asked by the first disciples to teach them to pray.

Prayer would not be worthy of being called a *spiritual* practice if it did not play a central role in this deep inner work of transformation. Perhaps you have never thought of prayer in these terms. I certainly didn't for a long time. I was quite content to think of it as spiritual work but never considered that it might be the means through which God gained access to me to do the spiritual work of transformation. This has not only changed how I understand prayer, much more importantly, it has changed how I understand my role and God's role in the whole process.

If, however, you happened to notice the subtitle of this book, you might wonder how the ancient monastic practice of *lectio divina* connects to this transformational dimension of prayer. Anything coming to us from a monastery might strike you as quaint but irrelevant to twenty-first-century Christians living busy lives in the world. But this could not be further from the truth. For, as we shall see, this ancient prayer practice was developed expressly for transformational purposes. It was understood as a way of opening ourselves to God so we might be touched, awakened, realigned, integrated and healed. Or, we could say, it is a way of opening ourselves to God so we might be born again and again in a continuing series of conversions that together constitute this grand process of transformation. This is precisely the gift that *lectio divina* offers us. It leads us to a way of understanding and practicing prayer that is vastly different from how most of us understand and practice it, because it leads us to opening ourselves to God so God can pray in and through us.

Be prepared, therefore, to have your understanding and practice of prayer changed. In fact, if you are not open to this hap-

14

pening, save yourself the time and put this book down. It isn't
for you. If, however, you seek a deeper openness to God and
long for God to continue the divine work of making all things
new—in you and in the world—then read on. If this is you, you
are the reason I wrote this book. I wrote it to help you see how
much more prayer is than you could ever imagine—how things
you may have never considered to be prayer are, in fact, ways of
opening yourself to God. I wrote it to help you move from
prayer as something you do—or, worse, feel you ought to do—
to prayer as a way of living your life. I wrote it with the prayer
that you and I would both not simply become people who pray
but people for whom our lives are prayer.

MORE THAN YOU
CAN IMAGINE

IF WE ARE HONEST, MOST OF US HAVE to admit that prayer is often more of an obligation than something arising spontaneously from desire. Part of the reason for this, I think, is that prayer is frequently presented as a spiritual discipline. Disciplines are things that we do not naturally do but feel we should do because they are supposed to be good for us. As you will have noticed, most children don't need to be told to play. It is only adults for whom play as a discipline might be necessary and potentially helpful! However, as we will see, prayer is the natural language of the soul. So there is something seriously wrong when it feels like something we should do.

But our problem is deeper than merely thinking of prayer as something we should do. The real problem and the core of the misunderstanding lies in thinking of prayer as something that we *do*. Understood more correctly, prayer is what God does in us. Our part has much more to do with consent than initiative. That consent, as we shall see, is most simply saying yes to God's invitation to loving encounter.

Prayer is so much more than we could ever imagine because God is so much beyond what we can ever contain in our understanding—even in our imagination. This is why the apostle Paul prayed to the God who, "working in us, can do infinitely more than we can ask or imagine" (Ephesians 3:20). And it is why Jesus, in the Sermon on the Mount, encourages us to think of the incredible beauty of a field of wildflowers when we worry about what to wear (Matthew 6:25-34). His point is that since not even Solomon was clothed in regalia as splendid as those wildflowers, we should trust that, since this is how God clothes the grass in the field, God's care for us will be even more unimaginably extravagant.

Prayer includes saying things to God—either silently or vocally, whether this be worded petitions or intercessions that we put together ourselves or formal prayers that have been written by others. But it is so much more than this. It can also include

- reading a passage of Scripture and listening for God's personal word to you in it
- meditatively walking the stations of the cross
- lighting a candle in church or your home
- allowing music to draw your spirit toward God's Spirit
- affirming your beliefs by reading or reciting the creeds
- reviewing your day and noticing where and how God was present to you in it
- meditating on Scripture and thinking about its meaning for your life
- fingering beads as a framework for meditation

- allowing your hunger during a fast to draw your attention toward God

- recalling your blessings and responding with gratitude

- subvocal repetition of a mantra (e.g., "Come, Lord Jesus" or "My God and my all") that moves prayer from consciousness to the unconscious and from mind to heart*

- celebration of the Eucharist (Communion)

- going for a long, rambling walk while repeating the Jesus Prayer ("Lord Jesus Christ, Son of God, have mercy upon me, a sinner")

- confessing your sins and asking for forgiveness

- smelling incense during a liturgy and having your spirit drawn toward God

- a contemplative walk in the forest that moves you from self-preoccupation to God consciousness

- making the sign of the cross or bowing before an altar or crucifix

- sitting in silence—allowing your heart to be drawn back to God by the periodic gentle repetition of a love name for God

- reading liturgical or other written prayers

- meditatively speaking the Lord's Prayer

- attending to your breathing—drawing in God with each inha-

---

*I discuss mantra prayers in chapter seven. But in case you are surprised to see this term applied to a form of Christian prayer, I should quickly say that, as we will discover, these prayers are Christian in content even if the form is most commonly associated with non-Christian religions. They are a deeply Christian way of being prayerfully open to God.

lation and releasing God to the world with each exhalation

- allowing your mind and spirit to turn toward God as you hear church bells or see a lit candle or any of an infinite number of reminders that can call your attention back to God
- singing or pondering the words of a favorite hymn or song
- meditating on an icon or a work of biblical art
- allowing your heart to soar in unworded praise in response to a sunset, a storm, a flower or a tree

Some of these may seem strange to you, possibly so far outside your spiritual comfort zone that you may wonder if they are worthy of being called Christian prayer. But all have been richly rewarding for Christians across the major divisions of the church and across the centuries of Christian history. All therefore are Christian forms of prayer, and because of this all have much to teach the person who desires to be attentive and responsive to God.

However, it is very important that we acknowledge that none of these things is automatically prayer. Nor, even, is addressing words or thoughts to God automatically prayer. But all these things—actually, all of life—can be prayer when offered to God in faith and with openness. It is the underlying orientation of the heart that makes something prayer. Without a heart that is open to God in faith, it may look like prayer and it may sound like prayer, but it won't be genuine Christian prayer. Genuine prayer always begins in the heart and is offered by an act of opening our self as we turn toward God in faith.

The ways God can communicate with us are infinitely more creative and diversified than we could ever imagine. Because of this, the ways we can communicate with God are correspondingly broader and richer than most of us ever experience. Growth in prayer is learning to open more and more of our selves to God.

PRAYER AS CONVERSATION

But what is prayer? The answer I was given as a young child was that prayer is a conversation with God. To encourage me to practice such conversational prayer, my parents gave me my first book on prayer for my thirteenth birthday. It was called *Prayer: Conversing with God*, and in it I learned that prayer could be as simple as speaking, silently or audibly, to God—just as I did to other people.[1] This was quite a powerful awareness. It became the foundation of a practice that has served me extremely well since then, the practice of frequently talking with God as I go through my day. Often this is a quick prayer of intercession, asking God to bless someone who comes to mind or whom I encounter. Or it may take the form of a few words of gratitude as I become aware of some blessing—like, for example, just now as I thanked God for my parents, who gave me that book on prayer, and for its author, who taught me so much. Sometimes it involves only a single word—*Help!* But, regardless of its length or content, what I have learned through conversational prayer is that my relationship with God is strengthened as I speak with God throughout the day because it reminds me that I am, in fact, in relationship and that God is with me no matter where I am or what I am doing.

I must say, however, that it took me a long time to begin to truly treat the interaction as conversation. For decades my prayers were nothing more than a monologue. I did all the talking, and I never once considered that God might be doing more than listening. The problem was not with my understanding of prayer, but that I didn't take it seriously enough. If I had really believed that prayer was conversation, I would not have been nearly as rude as I was. I would have talked less and listened more.

The good news is that God is ever reaching out in self-revealing love and has no more ceased being Revelation than being Love. The prayer conversation always begins with God. It does not begin with us. Prayer is our response to a divine invitation to encounter. The prayer conversation has already begun because God has already reached out, seeking our attention and response. Until we learn to attend to the God who is already present and communicating, our prayers will never be more than the product of our minds and wills. But prayer has the potential to be so much more. It can be the response of our spirit to God's Spirit as we open the totality of our being to the God who resides in our deep center and longs to meet us there.

The problem with understanding prayer as conversation is that prayer is so much more than communication. Reducing it to conversation makes it simply a mental activity—words and thoughts being a product of the left hemisphere of the brain. Prayer includes the mind, but is not limited to it. God invites engagement with more of our brain and more of our being. The glorious truth is that I can be praying to God without speaking to God, or without even consciously thinking of God. If this wasn't true, how could we ever hope to realize the ideal of continuous prayer that is encouraged in Scriptures (1 Thessalonians 5:17; Ephesians 6:18)? Obviously we cannot be thinking about God all the time. Nor can we be talking to God all the time. But prayer can be as foundational to our daily life as breathing. It can become a part of living, not just a religious practice or a spiritual discipline.

PRAYER AS COMMUNION

A better starting point for an adequate understanding of the breadth of prayer is to view it as communion with God. Communion includes conversation but is much broader. Because it involves union, not just closeness and connection, it also entails much more intimacy than mere conversation. We are, as Paul reminds us, in Christ, just as Christ is in us. That language reflects the intermingling that is part of true communion. It does not get much more intimate than this—an intimacy that is based on the reality of a mystical union with Christ, in the present moment, not simply something to be hoped for in the future. Our experiential knowing of this reality may be limited. But the union is real, even now. And the communion that we can experience in prayer is also real—so real that, more so than anything else that I know of, this prayer communion has the power to transform us from the inside out.

The good news is that we do not need to be talking to God or even thinking about God to be in prayer. We can simply be with God. That is the nature of communion. It is not dependent on constant communication. Think, for example, of being with someone you love and with whom you experience deep communion. Words are undoubtedly part of your being together, but notice how easily they can also fall away as you slip into a comfortable experience of simply being together in unworded presence. The same can be true of prayer.

Love makes this possible, and it is love that makes prayerful communion so fulfilling and transformational. Communion with God is the answer to our heart's deepest longings, because

God is love. Prayer is a relationship. It is dialogue that is based on a deep personal encounter. And since God is love, God can only be truly encountered in love.

PRAYER AS BEING IN LOVE

We might say, therefore, that prayer is being in love.[2] We can understand this in two ways, both of which are true, and each points to the other for its fullest understanding. In the first sense of this phrase we could say that prayer is being in love with God. As noted by John of the Cross, since God is love, God can only be known in and through love. Communion with God leads naturally, therefore, to a deepening of our knowing of God's love for us and, in return, our love for God. But speaking of prayer as being in love also reminds us that in prayer we come to know our being-in-Love. Prayer is not simply what we do. It is a way of being. More specifically, it is resting in the reality of our being-in-God. This is our fundamental identity. It is the hidden but deepest truth of our existence. Our being has no meaning apart from its relationship to God's being. The only possibility of being who I most deeply am rests in the eternal *I AM*. Because of the *I AM*, I can be. Because the eternal *I AM* is love, I can experience communion with God in love. This is what makes it possible for me to become truly and fully human, for me to become truly and fully who I am in Christ. And doing so has everything to do with prayer—not simply something I do but as a way of being in love, being in God.

This is why Teresa of Ávila says that the important thing in prayer is not to think much but to love much.[3] The head is not a bad place to start our prayer journey. But if prayer stays there too long and does not begin to sink to the heart, it will inevitably become arid and frustrating. However, when we allow prayer to begin to seep from our minds to our depths, it gives God access to those depths. Then, and only then, can prayer spontaneously emerge as God's action in us. And when it does, prayer becomes the overflow of the living waters that spring up from our depths. It becomes us listening in on a loving conversation of God with God as that conversation passes through us.

Our relationship with God may not begin in love, but it never deepens significantly until we enter into a personal encounter with Love. The more our being is grounded in God's love, the more prayer begins to flow from our hearts, not simply our minds. This is why Paul's prayer was that we might know the depths, breadth, length and height of God's love so that we may thereby be filled with the utter fullness of God (Ephesians 3:14-19). Christian prayer is a personal encounter in love, with Love. It is loving communion with the source of all love, with the source of our very being.

Perhaps you have heard the apocryphal story of a man I will call Juan. Every day near dusk Juan would stop in a church on his way home from his work—hardhat in hand, often dirty or at least dusty, and obviously tired. He would sit quietly in the back of the church for five or ten minutes, then get up and leave. Seeing him do this day after day, month after month, the parish priest approached him one day as he was leaving and told him he was happy that he used the church in this way. Juan thanked the priest for leaving the church open so he could come in, saying that this was a very important time for him each day. The priest asked him in what way it was important. Juan replied that this was his time with Jesus. He went on, "I just come in, sit down and say 'Jesus, it's Juan.'"

"What happens then?" the priest asked.

"Well," he replied, "Jesus says 'Juan, it's Jesus,' and we're happy to just spend some time together."

Juan may not have known it, but he had come to know the essence of prayer. He loved God and loved to spend time with God. Prayer is not simply a presentation of petitions, although bringing requests to God is certainly a legitimate and important part of prayer. Nor is it a discharge of an obligation. In essence, prayer is being with the Beloved. It is relationship. It is accepting God's invitation to loving encounter. It is, therefore, more like an echo than a self-initiated action. It is consent to God's action in our hearts and in the depths of our being.

JOURNEYING INTO LOVE

As our love journey with God develops, so does our prayer. It cannot help but do so because prayer is right at the heart of our relationship with God. Prayer is God's action in us. Our part is simply to allow divine love to so transform our hearts that love of God will spring forth as a response to love, not as the fruit of our determination.

The route to a life of prayer as loving personal encounter with God is to allow prayer to be God's responsibility. We can no more manufacture a genuine encounter with love than we can transform our hearts of stone to hearts of love. For these matters we can do no other than turn our face toward God and receive the love for which our souls so desperately long.

The Christian spiritual journey is responding to God's invitation to personal encounter in love. Prayer is our response. Prayer is the place of the encounter. Growth in prayer is growth in loving intimacy with God.

Thomas Green compares the stages of this growth to the stages in the development of a romance.[4] The first stage of prayer, he suggests, is the courtship—getting to know God. Since we cannot really love what we do not know, a love relationship must start with knowing the beloved. In the case of knowing God, this might begin with prayerful meditation on Scriptures. It might also involve using our imagination to meet Jesus in the events of his life on earth and seeing ourselves, with our own concrete personal history, connected to those events. At this stage, the goal of prayer is getting to know the God who is courting us.

The second stage of prayer is the honeymoon. Here we experience a transition from knowledge to experience, from head knowing to heart knowing. Meditation now slowly begins to require less effort. Our hope begins to be realized and the experience of God begins to flow freely with less meditative labor. We experience joy in just being with the Lord—just as good friends find joy simply in being together. They don't plan their conversation or analyze their relationship. They don't really even think about each other much when they are together. They are just happy to be together, whatever may be happening. This is Juan and his Lord.

Following the honeymoon, the third stage is what Father Green calls the movement from apparent love to true love. This corresponds to the long years of daily married life. And just as mature marriage relationships involve both a growing friendship as well as periods of deadening routine and at least occasional conflict, so too the prayer journey will inevitably include both consolation and desolation. If you don't know about desolation in prayer, you haven't been praying for very long. I have certainly known long periods when it felt like my prayers were simply echoing in my head but not reaching God. But, as we shall see, even desolation has its divine purpose. For here, in these periods of dryness in prayer, we can learn to drink deeply from the living water in ways that are not dependent on our senses. It is in these dark nights that our soul can learn to see by faith, not by sight.

MORE THAN YOU CAN IMAGINE

Prayer is more than you could ever imagine, because God is so much beyond what you can conceive. We are surrounded with gods that are too small to be up to the task of holding our deepest personal longings, never mind the world's most urgent problems. Our childhood God will never be adequate for those tasks. The ways of understanding and relating to God that we acquired in home, church and community are often seriously limited, sometimes dangerously wrong. This is why it is so important that we allow our views of God to grow and develop.

The view of God that counts in this regard is not the official one you might profess if you are trying to be safely within the lines of orthodox dogma. It is the one that is actually at the core of your experience of God, the one that underlies your experience of life. This will usually be the God of your childhood. For good or bad, this God is usually astoundingly robust—even in the face of later adult teaching that may demonstrate how incompatible this God is with the one you meet in Jesus. I think, for example, of the many people I know who live under an enormous burden of guilt that is associated with a harsh, punitive deity encountered in their childhood. Nowhere feels safe from the lurking presence of this God made in the image of parents or religious authority figures. Perhaps even more common are the large numbers of people—men and women—who have difficulty relating to a God that seems so inescapably masculine. In both situations prayer will be powerfully shaped by these views of God that are the residue of childhood teaching and experience—not shaped by the reality of the God who actually invites loving communion.

I have been speaking about the love of God and so have already drawn some attention to the implications of grounding our view of God in grace. I will have more to say about this as we proceed, but let me offer a brief comment on one dimension of our view of God that has great potential to limit our experience of God—namely, the gender of God. I comment on this matter not to argue a theological point but, in keeping with the thrust of this book, to draw attention to implications for prayer that flow from how we view God.

I have long been sensitive to the apparently exclusive masculinity of God, not because I had a bad relationship with my father but probably because I had a good relationship with both my father and my mother. My childhood oriented me to a God who was the source of both males and females and who was imaged by both. However, I related to God as male because the Father, by title, made it hard to think of anything else, and Jesus seemed inescapably male—even if far from stereotypically so by either first- or twenty-first-century cultural standards. This resulted in some intellectual puzzlement about how a gendered God could be the source of both males and females, but much more importantly, it left the parts of me that related best and most fully to women out of my prayer dialogue and divine encounter. How excited I was when I discovered the ancient Christian tradition of recognizing in the Spirit the feminine elements of the Godhead. This was far from a mere theological novelty for me. Immediately it began to influence my prayer experience. In the decades since this I have learned to bring more of myself to the God who is much more than either male or female, but who contains both. Sometimes I pray to the Spirit of God, who I view and relate to as female. But at least as often I pray to the Father or to Jesus, both of whom remain, in my mind, as male.

I do not think that the Holy Spirit is female, nor do I think that God the Father is male. God is beyond gender and at the same time the source of our gendered being. But, as I have allowed my ways of relating to and thinking about God to broaden, my prayer experience has correspondingly become much more than I could ever have imagined. I do not believe that my ideas of God, or any ideas of God, completely capture or adequately represent ultimate mystery. That is why I say I am making a spiritual point more than a theological one. And that point is that God is more than we can conceive, so we need to be careful to hold our conceptions with humility and gentleness so as to allow our prayer experience to not be limited by them.

MAKING IT PERSONAL

But enough of my prayer experience. Let's turn to yours. Perhaps your prayer remains more duty than devotion, more a matter of the head than the heart. Perhaps you know little or nothing of the sacred romance I have discussed. Don't be discouraged by this, but just as important, be careful to not allow yourself to become content with it. Remember that prayer is more a matter of consent than initiative. Trust that your prayer relationship with God has been established by God's initiative, not yours. Your part is simply making space for God, turning to God with attentiveness and openness. Don't think of this as an obligation. Hear it as an invitation to abundant and true life. Hear it as an invitation to the encounter in love that is prayer.

Settle for nothing less than knowing God in love. This begins by knowing the depths of God's love for you. All of us need to regularly return to this knowing. In fact, you can never get enough of it. Everything else that is required of you in life—your love of God, yourself and others—all flows out of your personal knowing of God's extravagant love for you.

Take a few moments, now or sometime soon, for prayerful reflection on the things presented in this chapter.

1. How would you describe your communication with God? Does conversational prayer—brief bullet prayers throughout the day—form a part of it? If not, consider if there may be a possibility here for deepening your relationship with God. How does God's communication to you form part of your dialogue? How might your prayer experience change if your times of formal prayer included more space for listening? What makes it hard for you to offer this stillness and silence?

2. To what extent is your experience of prayer an experience of loving communion with God? What things get in the road of this intimate knowing of God's love? What could you do to get yourself out of the way of what God desires to do in your depths to make prayer as loving encounter more of an experienced reality?

3. As you read the broad range of things that I suggested are part of Christian prayer, which of them seemed like they might be helpful for you? Perhaps it is something you already do and simply never thought of as prayer. What would change if you understood these moments as prayer? And what could you do to make space for more of these moments in your life?

4. Take some time to write out your own definition of prayer. Notice if your understanding of prayer has changed over the years and how that understanding has related to your practice of prayer. How did your childhood picture of God shape your practice of prayer? And how have any changes in how you understand God since then affected your prayer life?

5. Finally, if you haven't done so already, make a particular point of noticing anything in this chapter that seems to correspond to what the Spirit of God has already been teaching you or where the Spirit has been leading you. If you do nothing else, pay careful attention to this and respond to any invitations that you sense are coming to you from God. This too is prayer and is a particularly appropriate prayer posture as you continue to work through the following chapters.

PREPARING FOR
THE DIVINE ENCOUNTER

I RECENTLY HAD AN INTERESTING conversation with our
bishop about his meeting with Queen Elizabeth. It was far from
a private audience. He was part of the gathering of the eight
hundred or so bishops of the worldwide Anglican Communion
who were in England for the Lambeth Conference, all of whom,
with their spouses, were invited by the queen to Buckingham
Palace for a garden party. What interested me was the elaborate
protocol that had to be observed in this encounter, and the ex-
tensive preparation that was involved when a person is actually
presented to the queen. It made me think about what is involved in an encounter with God. Remarkably, the protocol for
the divine encounter is so simple as to be virtually nonexistent.
We are invited to turn up just as we are, and, as we will see,
there is nothing special that we need to do other than be our
self. However, preparation is helpful because being our self
with God is much harder than we might think.

TRUSTING OPENNESS

Openness to God demands trust. This is far from our natural posture—in relation to God or others. The natural posture of most of us is guardedness and pretense. The invitation to loving encounter with God immediately challenges this posture; God invites us to come in faith that expresses itself in vulnerability and brutal self-honesty.

Too often faith is reduced to beliefs. But cognitive assent to propositions has very little to do with genuine faith, which is more a posture of the heart than of the mind. Faith in God is leaning with confidence into God. The opposite of faith is mistrust, not unbelief. Faith is trust in God's goodness. This and this alone is what makes it possible for us to approach God with openness.

Prayer must start with faith because those who come to God must do so in faith. Apart from faith, Scriptures tell us that it is impossible to please God (Hebrews 11:6). Fortunately, however, we do not have to create this faith. It, and all else that God requires of us, is available as the gift of God. All that is required of us is the openness to receive what we can and then act on it. But we must act on what we have and be where we, in reality, are.

I have a friend who tells me that she is an agnostic—unconvinced of the existence of God and generally uninterested enough in the possibility to give it even a second thought. But, she tells me, from time to time she prays, usually when she finds herself thinking about questions of existence or the meaning of her life. I did not find the fact that she prays surprising, since I am convinced that prayer is a natural posture of the soul—something I will say more about later in this chapter. However, I was very interested in how she prayed. And so I asked her. She told me that usually her prayer goes something like this: "I am not sure if you are there, or, if you are, whether or not you are listening, or, if you are there and listening, whether I can trust you, but just in case . . ." Although my friend is not a Christian, this is Christian prayer. She is acting on the faith she has. It isn't much, but like the widow's mite and the generous act of giving that she displayed in the Gospel story of Jesus (Mark 12:41-44), my friend dares to give what faith she has back to God. Doing so makes it prayer. God will always hear any prayer that is born out of honesty and that expresses whatever amount of faith we actually have.

Trust and faith should frame our whole prayer experience. This is what allows us to let go of control and allow God to shape our prayer and our encounter. Prayer involves surrender to a mysterious inner process, submitting to something that God does in us. If we trust enough to let go, God will give us a gift of prayer communion that we could never create or even imagine. This is why we sometimes speak of prayer as Christ praying in us or as the Spirit making intercession for us. As the Australian Cistercian monk Michael Casey reminds us, "Prayer cannot be measured on a scale of success or failure because it is God's work—and God always succeeds. When we believe we have failed at prayer, it is because we decided what shape our prayer should have and are now frustrated that there is nothing we can do to implement our ambition. Prayer is nothing more or less than the interior action of the Trinity at the level of being. This we cannot control; we can only reverently submit."[1]

Our effort to make our prayers into the form we think they should be seriously interferes with this inner divine work of prayer. So does constantly examining our prayer to see how we are doing. The only thing we should seek in prayer is God.

When we focus on how we are doing or what we are getting out of prayer, we have taken our eyes off God and put them back on our self. But since the form that our prayer takes is God's business, we need to learn to mind our own business. Our job is to make space to turn toward God in openness and faith. God's job is the rest.

RADICAL HONESTY

I mentioned that honesty is part of the trusting openness that is involved in prayer, but I want to say a bit more about this very important dimension of true prayer. Part of meeting God in trust is being prepared to come to the encounter with nothing less than brutal candor. Thomas Merton reminds us that God is far too real to be met anywhere other than in reality.[2] Thus, when we attempt to meet God in our places of falsity and pretense, we should not be surprised that God is nowhere to be found. Where God will always be and where God waits to meet us is in the midst of the realities of our life and our experience.

Prayer is the encounter of the true self and the true God. This is what gives prayer its transformational potential. Honesty gives God access to the truths of our life, to the realities of our existence. Sadly, however, the self that we so often bring to God is our lying, false self—the self that we have defensively constructed to protect us from the vulnerability of our nakedness before God and in the world. God understands this vulnerability and our felt need for protection, but Jesus shows us another way to be in vulnerability and trust. This is the way of prayer. It was not simply what Jesus did when he addressed the one he called Father. It was the posture of his life as he offered his life as a prayer.

In prayer we speak from the hiddenness of our heart to the hiddenness of the heart of God. This secret place is where we find our true faces. In honesty before God we discover our voice and our true identity. But we must start where we actually are.

Preparation for prayer is asking for the grace to be real before God. This is something that we cannot do on our own. It requires grace—the gift of God that enables us to do what we most deeply need to do. God wants us to pray, and the gentle movement of God's Spirit within our spirit moves and enables us to pray. It is all of God. Our part is simply consent—opening our hearts to grace and allowing God to give us the prayer that we should pray.

Honesty before God is not simply avoiding lies. It is bringing our full self to God. Rather than trying to fix things up before turning to God, genuine prayer is turning to God in the midst of the mess that is the reality of our inner world. It is turning to God in the midst of our confusion and doubt, our anger, our hopes, our fears, our fantasies, our pain, our coping, our defenses, our struggles, our sin, and our brokenness. There is no cure for that which most deeply ails us unless we come to God with nothing held back. However, as noted by Vladimir Lossky, the good news is that every genuine presence of self before the face of God is prayer.[3] In prayer we can say anything, in any way, as long as it is honest—or more accurately, as long as it is as honest as, in that moment, we can be.

When we speak the truths of our lives in prayer, whatever they are and however we are moved to speak them, we are stripped bare of the multitude of deceits that infiltrate our being. Ann and Barry Ulanov comment: "Painfully, our values, even our best . . . are often exposed as values held with such possessive force that they have built a wall in us against the

force of God's will. But the defensive use of prayer soon falls by
the way if prayer really consists of honest conversation."[4] This
is prayer as divine therapy, a concept we will explore in the last
chapter of this book. Dare to stand before the naked God in
your own nakedness and you will be changed—stripped and
scourged, but healed, awakened and made whole.

THE LANGUAGE OF THE SOUL

Part of the preparation for prayer is coming to understand
what prayer is and what it isn't. One important aspect of prayer
that we have not yet addressed is that prayer is the soul's na-
tive language. Created in the image of God, our natural posture is attentive openness to the divine. Walking through the
primeval garden that was their home, our first parents were
ever alert to the presence of the God who shared their world.
Nothing was more ordinary than the extraordinary encounters they regularly had with the divine. Life was prayer. Prayer
was life.

But listening to the whispered lies of the serpent turns
everything upside down. Prayer no longer seems natural and
God no longer seems present. So, instead of the soul's normal
language of prayer as attentiveness, we create our own prayer
dialect—prayer as demand and control. Sometimes we offer
prayers to invoke God's presence or get God's attention. Other
prayers are designed to produce divine favors. And because we
are not really convinced that prayer is communion, our prayer
language involves endless chatter. We fear that if we are silent,
all will be silent. Words protect us from that potentially hor-
rendous discovery.

No longer as natural as breathing, prayer has become as
complicated as living. It has become something to do rather

than simply a way of being. Seldom is it merely walking through the garden of our day anticipating encounter with the divine Gardener. Prayer is opening the windows of the soul, receiving God's presence and enjoying communion with our Beloved. For this we were created.

Those who know God most deeply have relearned the soul's natural language of prayerful attentiveness to the divine. They are attuned to God. And they tell us that God is present and God is revelation. Personal experiential knowing of these two truths lies at the core of Christian prayer. No amount of words or actions can ever replace this knowing.

It is very important to remember that prayer is natural. If we do not, we will be easily seduced by suggestions that prayer must be learned and mastered. This sort of talk implies that prayer is a specialized skill—something most relevant to spiritual elites and professional pray-ers who have made it their life's work. (I think of the man who told me that prayer was what clergy are paid to do!) This is a serious misunderstanding. Prayer is for all of us and is as natural to us as breathing. It is, in fact, the breath of the soul. It is essential that we pray, just as it is essential that we breathe. Breath-holding can be hazardous to our physical well-being—even fatal! Prayer withholding can be equally hazardous to our spirit and soul. Don't pray because you should. Pray because you can and because it is as natural a response of your soul as releasing the breath that now fills your lungs—and then drawing in the next one.

DISCOVERING YOUR NATURAL PRAYER DIALECT

But if prayer is the natural language of the soul, each of us has a dialect that is most natural for us. Pause and reflect on what your natural dialect might be.

Perhaps it is silence. For many of us, words fall away when we are truly still before God and when we are most naturally and fully ourselves. But maybe your natural dialect involves words. Maybe when you are most deeply yourself with God what emerges are your petitions and intercessions, your gratitude, your praise, or your questions for God. Possibly your natural prayer dialect is more active than reflective or verbally expressive. Maybe being honestly your unique self before God takes the form of acts of loving service or social justice. Or perhaps it is more creative; possibly what bursts from within you when you are your true self before God is a short story, a dance, a wonderful culinary creation or a fresh way of looking at some important issue.

Each of us has our own voice, our own natural prayer dialect. As we will see in chapter three, holistic prayer involves starting with this and then expanding our range of ways of being with God so that our whole self, not just the comfortable parts of our self, are able to participate in the encounter. If we only stick with the most natural ways of opening to God, we will limit the depths to which we open our total self to God. Growth in prayer is learning to open more and more dimensions of our being to God—learning to commune and converse with God in ways that move us beyond those that come most naturally.

But back to that pause that I suggested—and which I will encourage you to take at various points in what follows. Take a few moments and be with God in the way that reflects your natural dialect. Allow your soul to speak in its natural dialect. Honesty also includes authenticity. Be with God in the way that is most naturally your way. And then, after a few moments, pick up the book again and continue to read.

HIDDEN PRESENCE AND DARK WATERS

Part of both openness to God and preparation for prayer is being ready to meet God on God's terms, not ours. This also is a gift of faith. God cannot be conjured up on our terms and under the conditions of our choosing. In fact, the reason God so often seems hidden and silent is precisely because we are looking in the wrong places.

John the Baptist proclaims that Christ stands in the midst of those who seek him, but we do not recognize his presence (John 1:26). This is a judgment that echoes across the ages. The presence of Christ is a hidden one, and it always will be. Only when we give up fashioning God in our image and seeking God where we think God should be, only then will we truly perceive the Christ who stands in our midst. Louis Evely writes, "God's most insistent call to us will always seem a sort of silence, since his language isn't ours. It isn't what we expect. Only when we love him enough to prefer his ways to ours, his language to ours, and his will to ours, only then will we discover him."[5]

Not a moment passes but Christ stands in our midst, and we fail to see him. Remember his words: "I was hungry and you gave me food, I was thirsty and you gave me drink, I was a stranger and you made me welcome, lacking clothes and you clothed me, sick and you visited me, in prison and you came to see me" (Matthew 25:35-36). God is present. But we must be prepared to allow God to arrange the encounter. The divine rendezvous must always be under God's control. The seeking, reaching out and communicating always begin with God. But we must be prepared for the fact that God will not be where we often might expect.

Prayer is not a magical ritual that allows us to bring the divine under our control. It is much more like floating on the dark river of God's love. You may not be sure where the river is taking you, and it will require that you surrender your control over the journey and the relationship, but one thing you need never doubt—the Lord of love has arranged the prayer rendezvous.

But let's be honest about this. Genuine openness to God can be a scary thing—particularly when the river we are asked to float in is dark, as it often is, and God's presence so often is a hidden one. If you have any doubt whatsoever about the depth and persistence of God's love, it is hard to trust yourself to stop thrashing about and simply float. The tricky part about floating is that you can't see where you are going. You have to swim in order to get your head far enough out of the water to see around you. That's why floating demands trust. Not only do you have to trust that the current is taking you in a direction that is ultimately one of blessing, but you also have to trust that you will stay afloat and won't bump into anything dangerous.

This is why genuine openness to God must start with a deep assurance of God's love for you.[6] Without this, you will be forced to try to stay in charge of the prayer encounter—your head will be out of the water all the time as you look around, trying to see where the river is taking you. Knowing the heart of the God who arranges the prayer encounter is essential if you are to dare to receive the gift of genuine openness to the divine.

Openness to God is simply a response to the hunger that God places in your heart. Any openness to God that you experience is a gift. Don't try to generate more. Simply ask God to increase your awareness of the depths and extent of your spiritual hunger—the yearning of your spirit for God's Spirit. God will do the rest, and prayer will flow from your heart.

BEING REALISTIC

It is important, however, to be realistic about what prayer involves. Followed long enough, the prayer journey will always take us not just to the mountaintops of spiritual consolation but to the aridity of desert desolation. But our Beloved has not abandoned us. Rather, we are being led to a place where we can learn to discern divine presence and live by faith, not just by the senses.

Instinctively, I prefer oases to deserts. I tend to approach dryness in prayer as something to be overcome, a problem to be solved. How jolting to realize that if I am to be genuinely open to God, I must come to love the desert, even to prefer it to the oases. How disturbing to be reminded of the upside-down nature of the kingdom of God! But ultimately, how liberating it is to be told the truth. It is good news to know that the dryness that is so often a part of my prayer relationship with God is not my fault—not the result of sin or spiritual sloth. How good it is to know that this is within the divine plan, that this is where God waits for me and wants to be with me.

You might wonder, however, why God permits the desolation of spiritual dryness—or, even more puzzling, why God invites us to receive it as a gift of great value. Although we may wish it were otherwise, it is uniquely in times of spiritual dryness that we can learn that there is nothing we can do to control God or produce divine blessings. The blessings we seek can only be received as a gift and grace of the Lord. When the spiritual well runs dry, God is saying, "I am God. I must be the Lord of our encounter. You cannot turn me on and off like a water faucet whenever you wish."[7] According to John of the Cross, this frustrating independence of God is the best proof we have that God is God, not merely a figment of our imagination.[8] I think he is right. If God is simply a wish fulfillment or projection of our needs, which of us would wish to create such a frustratingly independent God?

By making us wait in the dark and dry places of our inner world, God increases our spiritual hunger and thereby enlarges the capacity of our soul for the encounter in love. Now we can begin to meet God as God, not as the container of our projections and disordered desires. Now we can begin to let go and float in the river of divine love. What God invites us to do in the dryness of the dark night is to offer simple faith. God asks that we let go and float unseeing down the river that leads to light. This is not as risky as it sounds. God's assurance of love and presence allows us to learn to be at peace in the dark nights of our spiritual journey, even when those nights seem interminable. This is the testimony of Scripture and is the testimony of our Lord himself. Learning to trust love even when our senses fail to give us the accustomed comforts that previously signaled divine presence is the way we receive God's gift of perfect faith—a faith that is no longer dependent on the senses and assures us of divine presence regardless of our immediate experience.

PERSONAL PREPARATION

Take a few moments to consider your own preparation for prayer.

1. How would your prayer experience be different if you truly believed that prayer is God's work in you? Listen again to the quote from Michael Casey: "Prayer cannot be measured on a scale of success or failure because it

is God's work—and God always succeeds. When we believe we have failed at prayer, it is because we decided what shape our prayer should have, and are now frustrated that there is nothing we can do to implement our ambition." Do you agree with this assertion? If so, what makes it hard for you to trust that God is at work?

2. How do you assess your own honesty in prayer? What would it be like to meet God in nakedness, just as you are—speaking the truths of your experience? God is in the midst of your present reality, whatever it may be. Begin your prayer by asking for the grace to be real before God. Then, dare to exercise whatever degree of faith you have by turning to God in the midst of whatever you are truly feeling and experiencing. Don't attempt to fix it or step aside from it and then turn to God. Speak your present realities to God and allow your faith and knowing of God to grow deeper as you meet God in these places of vulnerability and honesty. Remember that in prayer you can say anything, in any way, as long as you are as honest as, in that moment, you can be.

3. To feel safe with this sort of honesty requires that you trust God's goodness. How deep is your confidence in God's love? Your prayer life will be no deeper than this confidence. Knowing God's love does not come from simply trying to believe it to be true but requires that you meet that love in vulnerability. Act on the trust you have by turning to God with the honesty you can

offer and receive the gift of God's gracious and loving presence. This is where you will come to know God's love.

4. Finally, read Paul's prayer for you in Ephesians 3:14-19 slowly and contemplatively. Read it as God's prayer for you, God's deep desire for you. Then read Romans 8:31-39, where Paul speaks of his experience of God's love. Ask God for this to be your experience.

Remember that in prayer we must always begin where we are. Even the desire to pray is prayer. This means that you are praying this very moment as you read this book—that is, as long as your reading reflects an openness to God in faith, not simply curiosity or an attempt at diversion from boredom. Prayer must always start where we are because that is where God is—where we actually are, not where we think we should be.

It is also important to pray as we can, not as we should. Be realistic. If you have never spent regular time in intentional personal prayer, don't attempt to start with an hour or even a half hour a day. Match your desire to the possibilities that are present in your life at this point in time, and offer some space to God as a way of saying yes to God's invitation to encounter.

Your job, after making that space, is simply to turn toward God—opening yourself in trust. God's job is the rest. Prayer is easily ruined when we make it a project— part of a spiritual self-improvement plan. Rather than pushing yourself forward by resolve, allow God to lead you by desire. The most typical evidence of grace at work within us is not awareness of duty but awareness of desire. You can trust your deep desires because they are a gift of God. *The Cloud of Unknowing* offers a striking image of this when it speaks of God as having "kindled your desire, and fastened to it a leash of longing."[9] Pay attention to how the Spirit is kindling your desires. This is the source of prayer. Allow prayer to take the form that God gives you at this moment, and keep attentive to the leash of longing that will draw you further into transforming union with God.

LECTIO DIVINA AND FOUR
CLASSIC PRAYER PATHS

IF PRAYER IS SO MUCH MORE THAN we normally think, and
if the ways we can open ourselves in prayer are so much more
diverse than we normally practice, perhaps a map of the possibilities would be helpful. Thankfully, the ancient Christian monastic prayer practice of *lectio divina* gives us just such a map.

PRAYING THE WORD

Lectio divina—literally meaning "divine reading" but better
translated as "spiritual reading"—is a way of prayerfully engaging with Scriptures in order to hear God's personal word to
you. It comes to us from the earliest days of the church, with
roots in Judaism. Jews have always had two approaches to the
Torah. The first is analytical and seeks to discover the one ob-
jective, true meaning of the text. The second is more subjective
in that it seeks the deeper and more personal spiritual meaning. Both, of course, have validity and importance, but it was
the second that provided the soil out of which early Christians
developed *lectio divina*. In the third century, Origen used the

Greek phrase *thea anagnosis* (divine reading) to describe a way of approaching Scriptures for the purpose of finding a personal message from God. This practice became more widespread when the desert fathers and mothers made the Word of God the basis of their prayer lives, and shortly after this Saint Benedict made the practice of *lectio divina* central to Western monasticism. Until the twentieth century it was primarily associated with monastic spirituality, although it has been rediscovered by lay Roman Catholics since Vatican II and by Protestants through the more recent rise of interest in classical Christian spiritual practices.

Although it is often treated as a technique, *lectio divina* is not really a procedure or even a method—at least not a single method. It is more an approach and an expectation. It arises out of a desire to not simply hear the *words* of Scriptures but also encounter the Word behind the words. At other times and in other ways of engaging with Scriptures we may seek insights, eternal truths and precepts for living. But in *lectio divina* what we seek is not information or motivation but communion and union.[1] We seek nothing less than God. We attend to the Word as a way of opening ourselves to God and listen for God's living word to us. *Lectio divina* treats Scriptures not as a text to be studied or a set of truths to be grasped, but as the living Word—always alive and active, always fresh and new.

It is, therefore, not so much a way of reading as a way of listening. The listening posture that it encourages is more passive than active. Reading Scriptures in this way is reading (and listening) with heart and spirit open. Don't try to find something or make anything out of the passage. Wait for the gift that God has for you in it. Read slowly and reverentially, savoring what you hear and gently listening for the still, small voice of God that says, "This is my word for you today." It is listening for the voice of God, communicated through Scriptures and revealed by the Spirit. It is, therefore, prayer because it is an opening of self to God.

Preparation for this posture of prayerful listening begins by settling yourself in God's presence in stillness and silence. Psalm 46:10 reminds us to be still so that we might know God. Stillness is a precondition to deep knowing of God. And silence, of course, is only good manners since God is already communicating. There is a knowing of God that is only possible in stillness and silence, and so this is where we should start when we seek to open ourselves to God—before Scriptures or at any other time.

After settling yourself in stillness in God's presence, offer a prayer in which you ask the Spirit of God to prepare you to receive God's Word. This is the Spirit who inspired the writers of the Bible, and the same Spirit who dwells in you. You are asking, therefore, that God inspire you—that is, that God infuse the Word into the depths of your being.

This is the essence of *lectio divina* as it has come to us from the rich history of Christian spirituality. It certainly can be practiced in more complex ways—and I will describe those in a moment—but I start with it in its simplest form because this is the place I recommend that you start if you are new to this way of prayerfully engaging with Scriptures.

My discovery of *lectio divina* was a gift of God. I stumbled upon it when I had almost given up hope of meeting God in a genuinely life-giving way in Scriptures. At earlier points in my spiritual journey, devotional reading of the Bible had been a wonderful, rich channel for encountering God. But as I slogged through an extended dry period of time in my spiritual journey

a number of years ago, I eventually gave up private reading of
Scriptures because my ways of reading them were simply not
serving as a means of grace. Giving up personal Bible reading
didn't answer my longing to meet God more deeply, but it did
relieve the frustration of willfully hanging on to a spiritual
practice that no longer was bringing life.

I first encountered *lectio divina* in a book by Basil Pennington.[2] He described it as his most basic and important spiritual
practice. I was intrigued because it was clear that, far from a
discipline, this way of engaging with Scriptures brought him
life. Here and elsewhere he spoke of waking in the morning
expectant about and eager to receive the word that God had
for him for that day. The Eucharist and *lectio* were, he said,
the two places where he was most deeply touched by God.
Together with centering prayer, to which I was also first introduced in this initial encounter with him and Cistercian spirituality, these formed the framework of his day as a monk,
creating successive periods of prayerful stillness, openness
and receiving of the in-flowing life of Christ. I wanted what
he had. I knew I needed to find a life-giving way of again
learning to open myself to Scriptures and through them to
encounter God. And I knew that my life desperately needed
the stillness that would allow this encounter to be more transformational.

Over the years this simple practice has profoundly rejuve-
nated both my reading of Scripture and my experience of God
in prayer. It is not the only way I read the Bible, nor is it the only
way I pray. But it has made Scriptures fresh and personal once
again, and has helped me meet God in a way that is immediate
and vital. In short, it has brought me back in contact with the
Word, not simply with the Bible.

FOUR MOVEMENTS, FOUR PRAYER PATHS

If we look at this prayer process more carefully we can, however, see that *lectio divina* involves four components, or—as I prefer to call them—four movements. Rather than being a linear process that must be mechanically followed, they describe four dimensions of the rich and dynamic dance that is *lectio divina*. Let me initially describe them separately in their usual sequence, and then we will return to the more fluid way this dance with God actually unfolds.

As usually practiced, *lectio divina* involves reading and listening to a short passage of Scripture several times with ample opportunity for contemplative stillness between and within each reading. In the classical form of the method associated with Benedictine spirituality, the passage would be read four times with a slightly different focus for each reading. If I were guiding you through the process, I might say something like the following:

> Prepare now to hear God's Word to you. In this first reading, listen for the general sense of what is being communicated. Open your entire self to this process. Attend to the words you hear, but listen particularly for the word or phrase that stands out for you. Also notice any images that might form within you, or memories, sensations or experiences that might arise in your consciousness as you listen. Sit in stillness after hearing the words and allow the Word of God to form within you as you open yourself in attentiveness and expectancy to what God has for you.

After the first reading and a suitable period of silence, I might then precede the second reading with these words:

> Listen now to the same passage read a second time. This
> time allow yourself to ponder what you are hearing in
> both your head and your heart. Notice the thoughts that
> arise in response to the Word, and notice the movements
> in your heart.

Following the same pattern, I might then precede the third
reading by saying:

> Listen now to the passage a third time. This time allow
> yourself to respond to what has touched your mind and
> heart. This response may be worded or unworded, but it is
> prayer if it is offered with faith and openness to God.

Finally, after another period of silence, I might then say:

> Listen to a final reading and allow yourself to simply be
> with God in stillness. Rest in God and be with the God
> who has spoken to you through the Word.

There is nothing magical about this wording, nor is there anything fixed in the way the passage should be listened to in multiple readings. However, what I just offered draws on a framework for prayer that was first outlined by the twelfth-century
Carthusian monk Guigo II. He identified four stages of monastic
prayer and labeled them as *lectio, meditatio, oratio* and *contemplatio.* He taught that prayer is a journey from the biblical text (*lectio*) to inquiry (*meditatio*) to response (*oratio*) and finally to the
gift of God's presence (*contemplatio*). Guigo II interpreted these
steps in quite a linear manner. In fact, the image he offered was
of a ladder with four rungs. Disregarding this hierarchical orga-
nization for the moment, I suggest that what these four Latin
terms describe is four broad prayer paths—prayer as attending,
prayer as pondering, prayer as responding and prayer as being.

Lectio	Prayer as attending
Meditatio	Prayer as pondering
Oratio	Prayer as responding
Contemplatio	Prayer as being

Four movements of *lectio divina*

Lectio is prayer as attending. This should be the foundation of all prayer. Literally meaning "reading," *lectio* reminds us that prayer should begin as attentive openness and expectancy. In *lectio* we listen and wait for the still, small voice of God that will speak to us personally and intimately. We seek to hear a word or phrase that is God's word for us for this day. In faith we wait for God to speak through Word and Spirit to our spirit.

Meditatio, from which we get the English word *meditation,* is prayer as pondering. Now we reflectively chew on what we have received from God in *lectio.* While *lectio* involves the senses and intuition, *meditatio* is primarily a cognitive (head) and affective (heart) activity. "Cognitive" means it involves thinking. But thinking that is spiritually productive can never be restricted to rational, analytical thoughts. It is more like pondering or reflecting. Consider Mary, who after the remarkable visitation of the angel of God and the communication of unimaginably breathtaking news of the child she was to bear is said to have pondered all these things in her heart (Luke 2:51). *Meditatio* can never be simply an activity of the mind. It must also engage the heart. The pondering of *meditatio* combines head and heart.

Literally meaning "speaking," *oratio* is prayer as responding. After pondering God's word to us, our hearts are touched and our wills are stirred. *Oratio* is our response to this stirring of our spirit.

There are many forms that such response can take. It may be a worded response—what we often think of as prayer. But we may also prostrate ourselves in worship, light a candle, stand or sit in silence that makes space for gratitude, write our own psalm, paint a picture, sing, go for a walk, or many other things. What joy it is to learn to not only pray with words but also with our hands, feet and hearts! The word that we have received has now begun to touch our deepest self, and we respond from those depths.

Contemplatio is prayer as being. As you will have guessed, we get our English word *contemplation* from this Latin root. In *contemplatio* we rest in the presence of the One whose word and presence have invited us to a transforming embrace. Having touched both our minds and our hearts, the Word now leads us into quiet rest in the Beloved. This is a prayer of presence. It is prayer as being—a gift of being in and with God that allows our subsequent and very important doing to flow from this quite still center. It is the movement from conversation to communion.

Most broadly understood, *lectio divina* involves receiving God's revelation wherever it occurs. This means that there are other media beyond Scriptures that can also be engaged with in this same prayerful way. We can, for example, apply it to the reading of a book or article. In fact, it is very appropriately used when reading something devotional—say, for example, the book you now hold in your hands. But we can also open our senses and attend to God's revelation while listening to music, viewing a work of art, contemplating an icon, talking to a friend, listening to a sermon or watching a sunset. As Paul reminded the Christians in Rome, for the mind that is open and prepared to see, God is always there to be seen (Romans 1:19-20). God's revelation is particularly clear in that part of creation that most directly reflects the divine image and likeness—the graced person.[3] In our very selves, and in others, we can experience the loving presence of God and hear God's word to us. *Lectio divina* is not restricted, therefore, to reading a book. However, the most privileged hearing of the word of God will always be when we sit in prayerful stillness before Scriptures, particularly when we do so within Christian community.

HOLISTIC PRAYER

You will recall that Guigo II saw *lectio divina* as four stages of prayer. He pictured these stages as four rungs of a ladder by which we ascend to God. Unfortunately, this imagery fits all too well with the spirituality of ascent that we seem to want—a spirituality of progressive approximations to some spiritual goal we think will be attainable if we play by the rules. However, regardless of how it is often misinterpreted in this way, Christian spirituality moves in exactly the opposite direction. Christian spirituality is a spirituality of descent. It invites us to follow Jesus on a path of self-emptying surrender. The way of Christ is always the way of the cross. Good Friday always precedes Easter Sunday.

But the consequences for the understanding and practice of prayer of this sort of ladder of prayer forms are equally dangerous. It turns a rich dynamic prayer practice into something mechanical and linear. Organizing the four components hierarchically also implies that they have an order of importance. This has been part of the reason why contemplative prayer is often mistakenly assumed to be a "higher" form of prayer—suitable only for the spiritual elites who have mastered the lower levels of prayer. This is a serious misunderstanding. All four movements of prayer are equally important and are gifts of God for all Christians. None are limited to people of a specific gender, age, personality or stage of the spiritual journey.

People sometimes say to me that contemplative prayer is not for them because they are too extroverted, or that pondering prayer is not for them as they are not sufficiently intellectual or reflective. Some tell me that prayer that engages the heart is not for them because they are not particularly emotional. But once again these judgments are based on misunderstanding. Because each of these ways of engaging in prayer corresponds to a way of engaging with life, one will always be more natural than the others for each of us. However, all of us will benefit from learning to open each of these portals of our self to God in prayer. By doing so, God begins to take the underdeveloped parts of self and weave them together into our true self that is being formed in Christ.

Taken together, these four movements give us a picture of holistic prayer. Opening the self to God in its totality involves meeting God in mind and heart, the senses and imagination, stillness and action, meditation and contemplation. Holistic prayer involves all of our being. In prayer we bring our total self to God, and in prayer that total self becomes increasingly a whole self.

Rather than thinking of these four components as stages, I would suggest that you think of them as movements of the dance of prayer. This dance does not have to follow a preset order. Allow the Spirit to lead this dance, and allow it to unfold spontaneously. Sometimes it will include only one or two of the movements, and sometimes all of them. Don't worry, therefore, about the sequence of what happens once you step onto the dance floor, and don't try to control the process. Just open your heart to God and allow the Spirit to lead this dance of love in the way that is God's gift to you for the present moment.

SILENCE AND THE WORD

If we look more carefully we can see that this dance is even simpler than I have suggested. Its four movements can be distilled down to two primary ones—silence and the Word.

Both silence and the Word belong to the core of prayer. God's Word draws us into silence. It cuts through our words to the silent center of our heart. But severed from what Cynthia Bourgeault calls the "nurturing ground of contemplative silence," our engagement with the Word tends to become analytical and loses its transformational power.[4] Silence quiets our spirit and deepens our awareness of God and ourselves. But in the absence of the Word, silence becomes an empty void—a place of presence to self that is not anchored in presence to God.

The Word and silence belong together. Their rhythm is as simple and basic as breathing. We draw in. We let go in response. Then, spontaneously, we open ourselves and draw in once again. And just as naturally we then respond with release. It should be the same with the rhythm of these two core movements of prayer. First we open ourselves in faith and draw in God's Word, and then we rest in silence, allowing that Word to become life to us. We breathe God in, we breathe God back out into the world and into our daily life. All Christians need both movements. No one can specialize in either the Word or silence—ignoring the other—without consequences to the health of spirit and soul. To do so is like trying to only breathe in or only breathe out. Each leads to the other—at least if you want to stay alive!

Where should you start? I recommend starting with the Word. Open yourself in faith and take in the gifts and invitations you receive from God through the Word. Let the Word wash over you, just as water flows over you when you stand in a warm shower. Ponder it—with heart and mind. Allow yourself to respond to it. But then be sure to leave sufficient space in silence for the being that grows out of what you receive.

Dare to believe that God still communicates and that Scriptures can become God's living Word for you. Then, with prayerful expectancy, savor the words of a short passage of Scripture, seeking God's presence and personal word to you. Take the word or phrase that you receive as a gift of spiritual manna— daily bread from the Bread of life. Sometimes you will return to the text several times, either to further reflect on the word that God has given you or to seek some new gift. At other times, a single word or phrase will quickly come to you, giving you something to ponder, respond to and be with for the rest of the day. Don't be distracted by evaluation or comparison. Remember, the nature of your prayer experience is up to God. So, get your nose out of God's business! Simply content yourself with being in the presence of God by praying the Scriptures. This is the prayer of *lectio divina*.

MAKING IT PRACTICAL

Lectio divina has the potential to be such a dynamic and vitalizing force of God in our lives that I want to be very sure that I don't leave it in an overly conceptual place. What it offers us is a tremendously powerful yet very simple means of being with God in stillness before the Word, something that can and should become a part of the prayer life of every Christian. Therefore, let me draw together some practical things that you can do if you feel invited to make this prayer part of your own practice.

1. Place. Pick a place that you will use for regular times of *lectio divina*. Make this somewhere quiet that will support attentive openness to God. Consider having a candle available that you might light as a way of inviting the Light of the world to be present as you start. A crucifix or icon might also be helpful, although do not use them if they would put you in serious tension with your own spiritual tradition. If employed, these sorts of aids to prayer do not make the place sacred. Your intent does that—namely, your intention of being open to God in a prayer of stillness and presence before the Word of God. But they can facilitate your awareness of God's presence, and it is in this way that they serve as prayer supports.

2. Time. Be realistic as you think about when and for how long you will try to practice this prayer, but also plan on being regular. It may be that daily will work for you. However, do not feel that you need to start with this. Many people try to take this time of prayer three or four times a week. Remember, pray as you can, not as you ought. Similarly, be realistic about how long a period of time you might set aside for *lectio divina*. This may not be the only time you pray or the only way you pray. But do set a realistic amount of time that you will strive to make available for meeting God in silence and the Word. It could be as short as five minutes. Longer is better (ten to fifteen minutes might be ideal), but not always possible. Make it as frequent as you are realistically able and for an amount of time that won't leave you feeling rushed. Remember, you are responding to an invitation to communion with your Beloved. Don't turn it into a heroic activity.

3. A short reading. Recalling that this prayer need not involve sitting with a book, let me nonetheless suggest that you begin by grounding your practice of *lectio divina* in reading, and that you make the reading of a short passage of Scripture a regular part of this. Theoretically, any portion of Scripture could be suitable, but most people find that this way of praying the Word works best when you engage with a short psalm (or a few verses of a longer one) or a short passage from one of the Gospels. The Epistles also work very well. If you do not have a framework for daily readings, you might utilize one of the available print or online lectionaries that list daily readings.[5] Whatever you read, the important thing is to read it slowly and contemplatively, several times. Remember, this is not reading for content. It is contemplative listening with openness of mind and heart, the senses and the imagination. Don't attempt to cover some set amount of biblical text—making this, for example, part of a project for reading through the whole Bible. Rather, just take a small morsel of Scripture and expect God to give you a word or phrase from it that will nourish your soul and meet your present spiritual needs.

4. Listen for a word from God. In this context, a "word" does not necessarily mean a single word; it could be a phrase or even a short sentence. It means a meaningful message summed up in a few words. Notice the gentle touch that draws your attention, makes you stop and think, or stimulates a memory or a body sensation. Trust that this is God's word for you.

Margaret Silf compares the listening process in *lectio divina* to the tasting process in exploring a box of chocolates. Just as in sampling chocolates we try one and then another, returning when we have found the one that is most satisfying, so too in *lectio divina* "we read, or listen to, a passage of Scripture and try each word, each phrase, as it slowly passes before us. And when we find a phrase, a thought, an image, or a memory that moves us in some way, we hold onto it and let that become our prayer."[6] There is no need to try to analyze your reaction or to figure out why this particular word speaks to you. Just receive it as a gift.

Sometimes God may speak very directly. A word or phrase of the text may seem to virtually jump out at you. Other times nothing will be so dramatically obvious. And there will be days when God does not seem to speak at all. But just listen in openness and attentiveness. And if nothing in particular speaks to you in that special way, simply take a word or a phrase in faith and carry it with you for the day. It may be that it will speak to you more personally later, sometimes when you least expect it. Or it may be a word someone else needs. Regardless, when you have identified the word or phrase that is for you, simply allow it to become a gateway to an encounter with the Lord. Ponder it in your mind and heart and take it with you for the day.

5. *Respond.* Thank God for the gift you have been given and for God's personal word to you. And then allow your heart and head to lead you in a response. This might take the form of a worded prayer, but need not. You may feel drawn to write something in your journal, make a painting, listen to or make music, or call a friend. Whatever your response, it is a way of expressing the word that you have taken in and on which you have been pondering. It is a way of releasing that word into your life. It is, therefore, prayer.

6. *Be with God in stillness.* Finally, as your worded prayer comes to an end, simply be with God in stillness. Sit in silence in God's presence. Soak in the goodness of God's grace. Allow yourself to be lost in prayer, lost in God. Rest in the presence of the living Word. Don't worry if nothing noteworthy happens. Like Juan—the workman who stopped for daily stillness and prayer in the inner-city church—simply spend some time with your Lord. This experience of wordless quiet enjoyment of God is contemplation. Receive it as a gift.

Notice that you are ending your prayer time as you began it—in silence. Take this contemplative stillness with you as you move out into your day. And remain ever watchful, because the God who met you in this

> divine rendezvous will be watching for you and seeking more moments of loving encounter throughout the day. So stay attentive and open.

GLANCING AHEAD

One way to organize the diversity of the hundreds of specific prayer techniques and practices that are part of the rich heritage of Christian spirituality is to consider them from the vantage point of the four movements of *lectio divina*. This will provide the framework for the next four chapters in which we will examine each of these four faces of holistic prayer in much more detail. What we discover is that while each prayer practice is grounded in either attending, pondering, responding or being, most of them move the pray-er from that base toward the other dimensions of holistic prayer. As I suggested earlier, there is no fixed pattern to the movement through these four faces of prayer, nor do all need to be present in any single prayer experience. However, God wants to include all of us in this transformational encounter that prayer involves. This means that we should not be surprised that while we can start anywhere on this prayer wheel, opening ourselves to God will always invite a response from the totality of our being. The dance with the divine can start on any of the four movements, but over time it will always lead us toward this holistic response.

PRAYER AS ATTENDING

IT IS 3:20 A.M. AND I AM SITTING in church. I am surrounded by darkness that is softened only by the light of a single candle on the altar. In front of me are forty or forty-five monks in white cowls—their hoods up, covering their heads and hiding their faces. They sit in silence, stillness and expectancy. Together we wait for the beginning of vigils and the first reading of the day from God's Word. I am a guest at Saint Joseph's Abbey in Spencer, Massachusetts, here for a retreat. Unlike the monks with whom I share these days of prayerful attentiveness, I do not regularly get up in the middle of the night so I can hear God's Word. But doing so these days I am profoundly aware of how important it is to ground prayer in attending.

This is *lectio*. It is the prayer of listening, watching, waiting and seeking to discern the presence of the God who is not only always present but also always reaching out to us in love. We do not pray so that we can get God's attention. We pray so that God will get our attention. We pray so that, as our attentiveness to God increases, our souls may be shaped by the reality of God's constant, loving, self-revealing presence.

THE GOD WHO IS PRESENCE

Although we are often tempted to think that God is absent, in truth, it is we who are absent. If God were absent, we would not be. Our being is dependent on God's being.

God's presence is grounded not simply in the promises of Scripture but in creation. Creation was not simply an event at a discrete moment in time. When God called the world into being, God established a reality that was absolutely dependent on continuous, sustaining divine presence. This is why Thomas Aquinas argued that we should never think of creation as an event with a before and after. Creation is ongoing. It is now. It is the unremitting outpouring of the life of God—an outpouring that is essential to sustain all that is.

Rowan Williams, the archbishop of Canterbury, offers an analogy that I find helpful in understanding the implications of this. Think about a light bulb. We know that when we turn on the switch and the light begins to shine, this is made possible because of electric current. However, that does not mean that the power was around only at the moment we turned on the switch. On the contrary, he argues, "the light is shining here and now because the electric current is flowing here and now. In the same way, it is the 'current' of divine activity that is here and now making us real." He goes on.

> It should be a rather exhilarating thought that the moment of creation is now—that if, by some unthinkable accident, God's attention slipped, we wouldn't be here. It means that within every circumstance, every object, every person, God's action is going on, a sort of white heat at the center of everything. It means that each one of us is already in a relationship with God.[1]

Behind and beneath everything that is, and every moment of existence, is the outpouring life of God. It is not merely a figure of speech to say that God is closer than our next breath. God is in that next breath—and each one that follows, as well as every one that has ever preceded it. Apart from the *I* AM, we would not be. Because of the *I* AM, prayerful watchfulness can be a means of cultivating awareness of God's constant presence.

Listen to the experience of Hafiz, a fourteenth-century Sufi mystic and poet who had a profound awareness of God's loving presence. His poem is titled "Keeping Watch."

> In the morning
> When I began to wake,
> It happened again—
> That feeling
> That You, Beloved,
> Had stood over me all night
> Keeping watch,
> That feeling
> That as soon as I began to stir
> You put Your lips on my forehead
> And lit a Holy Lamp
> Inside my heart.[2]

A strikingly similar thought is expressed in the following verse from a famous poem of the ancient Hebrew poet David—a poem that Jews and Christians know as Psalm 5.

> To you I pray, Yahweh.
> At daybreak you hear my voice;
> at daybreak I lay my case before you and fix my eyes
>   on you. (vv. 2-3)

Notice the sequence. David dares to be attentive to God because he trusts that God is already attentive to him. He knows that at daybreak God is listening for his voice, watching for him. And so, in response, he watches for God and holds himself in readiness and anticipation of loving communion with this God who is reaching out toward him. All proper understanding of prayer begins by realizing that prayer starts with God communicating and attending. God leans toward us with attentive openness and invites us to respond with the same.

Like Hafiz, David knew this extremely important spiritual truth. God is present to us in love, and this presence can be known and can be part of our experience. Attending to this reality is prayer. Cultivating this awareness lies right at the very heart of Christian prayer.

NOTICING LOVING PRESENCE

God may be present, but how often are we aware of this precious personal gift? Sadly, for the majority of us the answer is seldom. Most of us go through much of our life oblivious to the God in whom we live and move and have our being—unaware that this same God who is our origin and our fulfillment is with us as we journey through each day. We behave as if we were deists, not theists. We behave as if God may have been present when the light switch of creation was turned on, but has been remote since then. We forget that the continuation of our being and of all existence reflects the continuing outpouring of the life and being of God.

The cultivation of attentiveness to God's presence should be the soil out of which all prayer arises. Ignatius of Loyola, the sixteenth-century founder of the Jesuit order known as the Society of Jesus, understood this clearly and encouraged his followers to take time each day for prayerful attentiveness to how God has been present to us in love and attentiveness to how we have responded to that presence. He called this prayer the "examination of consciousness"—or, in short, the examen. When blessed by God, it leads to a healing of awareness—a deep, inner transformation of consciousness in which awareness of God's presence increasingly becomes the constant background of our life.

There are three simple steps to the examen. Here is the way I interpret them.

1. After settling into a place where you are unlikely to be disturbed, begin by affirming that wherever you are, you are in the presence of God. Gather yourself together in stillness before God, allowing yourself to become aware of the God who is present within you, in the people God has placed in your life and in the world. Express to God your desire for the grace of seeing yourself, others and the world through God's eyes.

2. Now allow your attention to roam over your present day, letting the fragments of your day flow across your consciousness as memories. There is no need to try to organize or control these memories, or to attempt to be comprehensive in your review of the day. Simply trust that the Spirit will bring to mind the significant events to which you should attend. As this happens, notice the blessings of the day and give thanks to God for them. But also pay attention to the internal movements of your heart and your response to the people and experiences that were part of your day. Notice those times when you failed to see the face of Christ in someone you encountered, or you responded out of fear or personal interest rather than love. This is not the time to dwell on your shortcomings and berate yourself. Simply express sorrow for those moments in the day when

you failed to be aware of God's love and allow it to flow freely through you. Ask for forgiveness for the times you resisted light and chose darkness, and thank God for the times grace allowed you to be swept along by the flow of God's love.

3. Close by asking again for the grace to be open, attentive and responsive to God's loving presence, thanking God once again for this most precious gift. You might then finish your time with the Lord's Prayer (the "Our Father").

I often end my day by praying the examen. Typically I spend about five to ten minutes in this prayer. Usually I am aware of large blocks of the day in which I was unaware of God's presence and closed to God's inflowing life. It saddens me to see this, but acknowledging it helps me cry out for the grace to keep turning in openness and trust to God and the grace of seeing life through God's eyes. But these are also times of joy as I see the moments where I allowed myself to be open to and aligned with God's action in me and in the world. Let me give an illustration from a recent day.

The day in question was ordinary: most of it spent in front of my computer—writing and periodically taking a break to answer email—a late afternoon bike ride, dinner and some relaxed evening time with my wife, ending with a walk and a final check of my email. Like most days, my memory of the day that came to me during my prayer of the examen was disjointed—not sequential and far from exhaustive. (Imagine how exhausting it would be if it were exhaustive!) I let the snippets of the day float before me until suddenly something caught my attention. This night the first thing to do so was an email from someone upset by something I had said. As I focused on this moment, I reminded myself that my purpose in looking at it is not self-analysis but God-spotting. My question is where God might have been in this incident.

Suddenly, I smiled. The answer was all too obvious. What I saw was no longer a friend telling me of irritation in the face of my inappropriate harshness, but God gently inviting me to step aside from my drivenness and compulsive overachieving—inviting me once again to let go. My hurtful comment had arisen from my irritation that my friend was not living up to my own unreasonable expectations of myself. God was, in her, inviting me to choose life and again surrender my own ideas of what this involves and how to achieve it.

Encountering something like this makes it very easy for me, at this point in the examen, to be sidetracked by planning for self-improvement. But, remembering that what I really desired was knowing God's presence, I simply thanked God for this divine visitation and gift of grace, expressed regret over my hurtfulness to my friend, and then allowed my review of my day to continue. This was followed by more high-speed mental skimming over the surface of the events of the day. I repeated my intention to notice where else God had been with me in this day.

Suddenly another moment in it caught my attention. This time it was riding my bike through a wonderful grove of trees in a section of the bike trail near our home. I saw again the rays of sunlight passing through the branches of the tall Douglas-fir trees that surrounded me on the trail. I felt the warmth of the sunshine. I heard the cracking of the densely packed fine gravel of the bike path beneath my wheels. Again I smiled. I knew the gift of being alive in God's world, of being in God, of being with God. My heart was filled with gratitude. I thanked God for the joy of this Spirit-led recollection and perception. I didn't believe God had been with me. I knew it.

Suddenly I found the words of a hymn by Maltbie Babcock

coming to mind, followed immediately by the familiar tune I had first sung as a child:

> This is my Father's world, and to my listening ears
> All nature sings, and round me rings the music of
>   the spheres.
> This is my Father's world: I rest me in the thought
> Of rocks and trees, of skies and seas;
> His hand the wonders wrought.
>
> This is my Father's world, the birds their carols raise,
> The morning light, the lily white, declare their
>   Maker's praise.
> This is my Father's world: He shines in all that's fair;
> In the rustling grass I hear Him pass;
> He speaks to me everywhere.[3]

I thanked God for the blessing that this early-twentieth-century Presbyterian minister's prayerful attentiveness to God was to him, to me and undoubtedly to so many others. And then I allowed my review of my day with God to continue.

And so this time usually goes. Never does it involve anything like a comprehensive review of the whole day. But always it turns my attention toward my Lord. I find it a gentle and intimate way to end the day in prayerful communion. Sometimes I get temporarily lost in reflection on the events that the Spirit has brought to my mind, but usually, once I realize what is happening, I am able to set this aside and simply focus on my awareness of and response to God. Of course, in some transactions this is more difficult than in others. When I can't discern God's presence in an experience or memory, I simply pray that God will help me do better in the future. It is not my job to make something happen; all I am asked to do is simply be open to God in attentiveness.

Like any spiritual practice, the examen can be demanding. Although it does not need to take longer than ten minutes and can be meaningfully done in less, for the beginner these minutes can easily be a constant struggle with concentration. If this occurs, rather than try harder to focus your attention, simply follow each period of wandering thoughts with a gentle repetition of your intention to reflect on where God was with you in the day. Ask God to control the thoughts about the day that come to mind. And then trust that whatever does come to your mind is what you should examine with an eye to noticing where God was in that experience.

There is no need to wait for the end of the day to pray the examen. In fact, an ideal time to do so would be right now. Finish this paragraph and then set aside the book, taking a few minutes to allow the Spirit to lead you through an exercise of God-spotting in terms of this present day. Where has God been present to you in it? Thank God for these gifts, and pray that you might be even more attentive to and aligned with God's presence as this day moves forward.

PAYING ATTENTION

Learning to pay attention to God's presence and leading in the flow of our days is the foundation of a life of prayer—or, as we shall see in chapter eight—life *as* prayer. Our spiritual life will be no deeper than our capacity to pay attention. And our capacity to pay attention to God will be no greater than our capacity for and practice of paying attention to that which is within and beyond our self in the present moment.

Think about what it means to pay attention, and I suspect

you, like me, will be taken back to times when, as a child, you were told to pay attention by parents or teachers. The problem when children are apparently not paying attention is, however, not that they are inattentive but rather that they are attending to something other than what adults wish. When, as a child, this would happen for me, I was usually caught up in some interior world of imagination or preoccupation. What I was usually being asked to do was to focus on something that someone else thought was important—usually a task or an instruction. However, the kind of attention that is essential if we are to open ourselves to God is quite different from this effortful focusing of our thoughts and constriction of our imagination. In many ways it is the exact opposite. Prayerful paying attention is not scrunching up our willpower and tightening our focus, but simply opening our self to what we encounter. This makes it much more an act of release than effort. We release any attempt to control attention and instead allow it to be absorbed by our present experience.

This insight lies right at the heart of the profound spiritual wisdom found in the teaching and life of Simone Weil. No one has taught me more about what it means to pay attention as a way of being open to God. A French Jew born in 1909, Simone Weil was trained as a philosopher but subsequently spent most of her short adult life working in a car factory, laboring in the French vineyards, serving with the Spanish Republican Army on the Catalonian front and working with the French Resistance during the Nazi occupation of France—all while writing some of the most brilliant and profoundly spiritual books to emerge from the twentieth century.

Looking at her life from a distance we see only a woman whose radical commitment to truth and justice and her insistence on living in solidarity with the afflicted led to her premature death at age thirty-four. From that distance we get glimpses of only her passion and what might be thought of as her politics. But from this distance we fail to understand her life and the depth of her spirituality. Looking more closely, however, we see the most central principle of her life—the priority of paying attention. It was her lifelong commitment to the constant practice of attention that lay behind everything she did and was. This was also the core of her spirituality and, she argued, the core of what it means to live a life of prayer.

She described this attentiveness as detaching from her thoughts and leaving her awareness empty and ready to be penetrated by whatever she encountered. Attention, she argued, is the best preparation for prayer, and absolutely unmixed attention is prayer.[4] It is a state of active receptivity that opens us up to the sacred. Attention for Weil is not the active mental process of concentration that is involved in what we usually refer to as "paying attention." Rather, it is suspending our thoughts and allowing awareness to develop. It is therefore more like prayerful openness than thinking. In fact, she argues, "attention, taken to its highest degree, is the same thing as prayer. It presupposes faith and love. Absolutely unmixed attention is prayer."[5]

Paying attention is being open and awake—ready to be seized by whatever is present to us in the present moment. This is why it is a foundation of prayer. Attentiveness is prayer because attention paid to anything is a doorway to the self-transcendent. It moves us beyond our self-preoccupations and opens us to that which is beyond our self. Regardless of how insignificant the object may seem, being truly aware of anything has enormous potential to aid our spiritual awakening. Prayerful attentiveness is not, therefore, reducible to thinking about God.[6] It is prayer when it is offered with faith and openness to the God in whom everything that exists is held together. God interpenetrates every part of creation, and nothing exists in creation that is independent of God. Paying attention to anything, therefore, has the potential to open us to this God who is present in all life. Adapting an expression of Abraham Kuyper, there is not a square inch of reality in which God is not present.[7] Attentiveness to this presence is prayer.

Paying attention also demands that we be present to our self in the present moment. We cannot pay attention to something that is in the past or that may be in the future. We can remember things in the past or anticipate those in the future, but we cannot be present to them. We can only be present to that which is actually present. Consequently, paying attention is always an engagement with the now. This becomes prayer when it includes openness and presence to the God who is present to us now.[8] Where else would the Eternal Now meet us than in the present moment?

SENSORY PRAYER

Our senses offer us great help to be present and open to God in the present moment. Stop and take a minute to notice what you can sense right now—not think about, nor remember, but see, smell, hear, taste or feel on your skin. Doing so pulls you immediately into the present moment because that is where the senses operate. This is why the senses have such an important role in spirituality. They reconnect us to our bodies and ground us in the now.

Earlier I mentioned that lighting a candle can be a prayer. The way it does so is by drawing our attention to the God who is both wholly Other and Immanuel, transcendent and immanent, absolutely beyond us in all aspects of being but astoundingly present as we turn in faith and trust in the present moment. The flame, the crackle of the electric lighter or smell of sulfur from the match, the slight puff of smoke call us into the present moment and invite us to pause before this gift of presence. We do not turn to the candle, although it may be in our gaze. We turn toward God. And this turning in openness and trust is prayer.

Some Christians mistrust or deemphasize the role of the senses in spirituality, considering them to be inferior to reason and cognition. Such a view fails to appreciate the indispensable part of human personhood the senses actually form. It falls into the gnostic error of denying human embodiment. Because Christians affirm the goodness of the physical body and believe in the physicality of the incarnation, we should also affirm the importance of encountering God through our senses. God gave us senses to enrich our lives. They are channels that can be spiritually tuned so as to register the traces of the divine that saturate the world. Our senses can also be a way of calling us to attending prayer—inviting us to pause and turn to God.

Think of walking through a spring garden filled with the scent of flowers, or sitting by the edge of a stream, listening to the babbling of the water and feeling the gentle breeze of a summer afternoon. Soaking in these sensations can be prayer when it leads to a soaring spirit that is open to God. Or, if you have ever been part of a solemn High Mass, recall the sense of the ineffable presence of the Spirit of God that is associated with the billowing incense or the ringing of the Sanctus bell. Christian prayer invites the opening of the total self to God, and anything that involves such opening is prayer.

But there are many other events in our days that can serve as a call to attentive presence to God. Just as Christians in past generations used to stop for a moment of prayerful stillness when they heard the bells of the church ring the hours of the day, we can identify other sensory signals and use them similarly as a call to prayer. It may be that church bells ring throughout our day and we have simply not been hearing them. If so, we can join the generations of Christians who have used this reminder for attending prayer. But it could be the sight of a child, the sound of birds singing, the smell of flowers or freshly cut grass, or the feeling of warmth. Any of these things—and many more—can serve as a call to pause and, even if just for a moment, turn our heart toward God. With even just a little attentiveness, our lives will be discovered to be filled with things that can serve as this sort of a call to prayer if we truly seek to be open to the God who is present to us in the midst of our daily lives.

I am a sailor and so, not surprisingly, love the wind. I live in a place that has a steady ten-to-fifteen knot breeze blowing off the ocean most days. Almost every time I feel that wind my thoughts turn quickly and automatically to God. I draw in a deep breath, my spirit soars, sometimes I shudder and zip up my jacket, but almost always my spirit turns toward the Spirit. This hasn't happened automatically. It was aided by reflection on why my spirit soared in response to wind and the spiritual significance of wind and breath. God blessed those reflections by associating the sensation of wind with thoughts of the Spirit. This, for me, works much like the association of prayer and church bells that existed for medieval Christians.

Our senses are a call to attention and to presence in the moment. They are extremely rich spiritual resources for a life that is attuned to God. Allow them to turn your attention to God.

SPIRITUAL PERCEPTION

Attentiveness to God is a gift, not an accomplishment. God gives us all that God asks of us. This starts with faith and includes awakening and attentiveness. Paying attention is, therefore, a response to grace. It is the gift of seeing through God's eyes, hearing through God's ears. It is a gift of the Spirit of God healing our awareness and giving us a measure of the perceptual acuity of God.

I recall listening to a BBC interview with Mother Teresa not long before her death. When the interviewer asked her how she could persist day after day serving the lowest of the low on the streets of Calcutta, her answer was that it was easy when she saw Jesus as she looked into each face.[9] We can only truly see the things of God through eyes of faith, and eyes of faith are the eyes of God—God's gift to us of new possibilities for perceiving reality.

This takes us back to prayer as what God does in us. It is, as we are seeing, so much more than what we do—even what we do when we pray. It is also part of what is involved in taking on the mind of Christ. Often this is interpreted in overly mental terms—reduced to some sort of a cognitive realignment of our beliefs with orthodoxy. But the mind of Christ involves something much deeper than beliefs. It starts with Spirit-shaped perception. This is what allows us to see through the eyes of God and hear through the ears of God. It is what allows us to truly encounter the reality that our selective and limited perception normally excludes and distorts. It is what allows us to truly encounter God in all things.

Perception prepares us for response. When we encounter life through Spirit-shaped perception, we are prepared to respond as God would respond. Seeing Jesus in each face that presented itself to her made Mother Teresa's life quite simple. She simply gave to each as she would give to Jesus. Similarly, seeing injustice that we might otherwise choose to ignore impels us to respond as Jesus responded to injustice. Spirit-shaped perception graces us with the mind of Christ. It allows the Christ in us to guide our response.

I write these words on election day in British Columbia. The dominant issues in this election have been the economy and the environment. But I have just returned from a walk through downtown Victoria. Today, as most days, I was approached by half a dozen or so panhandlers. I also saw several homeless people asleep in alleys and one under a bridge. They challenge my inclination to vote in terms of my self-interests. They urge me to give social justice issues much higher priority as I consider who to vote for. They also urge me to align myself with God's action in the world and participate in the establishment of the kingdom of God on earth. This is the way the mind of Christ works. It shapes our perceptions and directs our actions. It was at the core of the life of Christ, and it is at the core of the life of all Christ followers who seek to make their life a prayer.

Seeing life through spiritual eyes also involves seeing the world through eyes of wonder, not simply through eyes of reason and analysis. This means it involves the renewal of the capacity to perceive and be touched by beauty. As John O'Donohue argues in *Divine Beauty*, "When we awaken to beauty we become aware of new ways of being in the world."[10] This too is prayer, and it is part of how taking on the mind of Christ leads us to places of deep healing and prepares us for vital engagement with life and the world.

CULTIVATING PRAYERFUL ATTENTIVENESS

But now it is time to make all of this much more practical. Let me offer four concrete ways to cultivate prayerful attentiveness. While, as I have said, such attentiveness is a gift, not an accomplishment, it is a gift that can only be received with intentionality. A gift must be opened to be truly received, and there are several important things you can do if you wish to receive the gift of this sort of prayerful attentiveness and allow it to become part of your life.

1. Make time in each day for pauses in stillness, using these moments for attentive prayer. Consider using some periodic event that occurs most days—for example, each time you look at your watch, pass through a doorway, or receive an email or other form of electronic message—as an occasion for a brief worded prayer to God in which you express your intention of being open in trust to God. You might find it help-ful to silently repeat a short phrase at this moment—something like "open and attentive" or "eyes to see" or "my Lord, my God"—a phrase that might become a personal mantra for you. The point is simply to use the regular events of life as a call to prayer—much as church bells used to call Christians or the muezzin still today calls out from the minaret of the mosque for Muslims. In this moment, simply turn toward God in trust, openness and attentiveness.

Another way of doing this is to start each time of worded prayer or each time of any other spiritual practice with a few moments of stillness before God. Use this time to simply gather yourself in stillness before God. Your prayer has already started if you offer these moments as gifts of unworded presence to the One who is present to you. Don't reduce your silence to a container waiting to be filled. Offer it as an expression of your intention of making space for God—space to be truly open to God's presence and communication. Remember that the prayer communion is God's initiative and work. And don't forget that God has already started the conversation!

2. Watch for traces of the divine in daily life. Nothing has the capacity to make all of life a prayer more than spiritual eyes that allow us to know the presence and action of God in us and in the world. Deep knowing of this reality transforms our consciousness—replacing the usual background noise associated with the endless chain of thoughts, memories and associations with a quiet, steady knowing of our being in God and our participation in the life of God. It also changes our identity as we come to truly know—not just believe—that our deepest and truest self is hidden in Christ. And it addresses our most fundamental need to know that we belong and that our life has purpose and meaning.

Make a regular habit of prayerfully reviewing your life. If you have never done this, start with looking back over the past day. Or, if you have a longer block of time, notice where God has been present in your life over the last few months, the last year or even your life as a whole. A good friend of mine recently spent the year before his sixtieth birthday making each of the successive five-year periods of his life the subject of his reflection for a month. For that whole month he asked God to guide his prayerful attentiveness to how God had been present with him during that five-year period, and then he journaled on it, allowing it to shape new understandings of himself and the newly emerging deeper awareness of the presence of God in his life. The process changed him in deep ways. That is what prayer does.

3. Watch particularly for traces of God in other people. Since humans are that part of creation most directly reflecting the divine image and likeness, it should be here that we most readily sense traces of God. Cultivate the spiritual habit of looking through Spirit-filled eyes at those you encounter and watching for Jesus. Recall that he said that he is there—particularly in those most broken and least likely to be suspected of bearing the Christ within their being. Watching for the presence of God in others will change the way you relate to them as you begin to see yourself surrounded by bearers of our Lord's presence in the world.

4. Consider taking a periodic spiritual retreat as a means of nurturing attending prayer. Spiritual retreats are times set aside for retuning our perception in prayerful stillness and solitude. The psalmist tells us to "be

still and acknowledge that I am God" (Psalm 46:10). Stillness is its own form of perception. It allows us to know things that can never be known under any other circumstances. It allows us to know the ground of our being—the I AM. Not everything that is called a spiritual retreat is designed to aid this knowing. Some retreats are filled with talking, teaching, planning and a variety of other activities that leave little or no room for solitude or stillness. These activities can, of course, have an important role to play in our spiritual life, but they are distracting to a spiritual retreat that is designed to nurture attending prayer. Such prayer requires a degree of inner stillness, and the sort of retreat that best supports its development is one that is grounded in solitude and silence.

Retreats are shaped more by the intention of our heart than their location or length. We do not need to follow Jesus to a desert for forty days. Our circumstances may only allow an afternoon or a weekend, and where we go is not crucial as long as it gives us an opportunity for some degree of stillness and solitude. Work with what you have available to you. But do not overlook the possibility of making your retreat at a monastery, convent or some formal retreat center. Here you usually have the added advantage of being supported by the prayers of the community you enter as they wait with you in expectancy of your encounter with God.

Jesus said: "When you pray, go to your private room,

shut yourself in, and so pray to your Father who is in that secret place" (Matthew 6:6). The private room to which Jesus invites us is not a physical place. It is an inner state. This is why Jesus said that God is present in this secret place which we enter when we shut the door to outer distractions and seek to open our self to God in prayer. It is in this secret place that we are hidden in God's presence. It is in this secret place that we can uniquely receive and learn to unwrap the gift of prayerful attentiveness.

Retreats are not simply times to meet God but times to find your way back to your inner private places of prayer. And don't forget, the best thing about these inner places of divine encounter is that they are totally portable. Wherever you are, and virtually whatever you are doing, provides opportunities for brief moments of retreat—brief moments of time in which you can turn your attention and open your heart to God. This is the core of Christian spiritual retreat and is the reason why retreats hold such potential for the awakening of attending prayer.

PRAYER AS PONDERING

IF YOU HAVE BEEN ACCUSTOMED TO thinking of prayer as talking to God, you may have been surprised to see the limited role of thought and words in attending prayer. Because we so easily become preoccupied with our thoughts, spiritual attentiveness requires that we learn to detach from them in order to apprehend that which can never be reduced to thought. But this does not mean thinking does not have an important role in prayer. Two of the four prayer paths we are considering give a prominent role to thoughts and words—prayer as pondering, to which we turn in this chapter, and prayer as responding, to which we turn in the next.

Cognition is far too important a part of what it means to be human to not have a place in prayer. Anselm, the eleventh-century archbishop of Canterbury, argued that the chief way humans show likeness to God (the *imago Dei*) is in our capacity for thought and language. Both, therefore, must be part of what we bring to any encounter with God that involves openness of our whole being.

PONDERING PRAYER

Our English verb *ponder* comes from the Latin noun *pondus*—meaning pound—which, when turned into a verb, suggests the mental activity of weighing or considering something. It is clearly a form of thought, but it is reflective, not analytical thought. When we ponder something we hold it lightly and give it space. We turn it over and consider it from various angles. We ruminate on it—that is, we think about it repeatedly, slowly and casually, efficiency of our thought process not being as important as carefully considering all aspects of the issue.

Pondering becomes prayer when reflection arises in a mind that is open to God. Consider the following prayer of David, recorded in the ancient Hebrew Psalter as Psalm 14.

> The fool has said in his heart,
> "There is no God."
> Their deeds are corrupt and vile,
> not one of them does right.
> Yahweh looks down from heaven
> at the children of Adam.
> To see if a single one is wise,
> a single one seeks God.
>
> All have turned away,
> all alike turned sour,
> not one of them does right,
> not a single one.
>
> Are they not aware, all these evil-doers?
> They are devouring my people,
> this is the bread they eat,
> and they never call to Yahweh.

They will be gripped with fear,
where there is no need for fear,
for God takes the side of the upright;
you may mock the plans of the poor,
but Yahweh is their refuge.

Who will bring from Zion salvation for Israel?
When Yahweh brings his people home,
what joy for Jacob, what happiness for Israel!

This is what I would call a pondering prayer. David is considering issues that are troubling him. This is not a dispassionate analysis of circumstances or events. It's a soul reflection on matters that bother him deeply. He is disturbed by questions that have no easy answer—questions, in fact, that have no answer at all. These questions must be lived, not simply closed off by some sort of terse conceptual response. They demand pondering—holding in a reflective space. And so this is what David does. What makes it prayer is that he shares these ruminations with God.

Pondering prayer is talking with God about our thoughts, our wonderings and our reflections on life experiences or challenges. In the prayer recorded in Psalm 14, David begins by commenting on what he observes around him. He feels that he is surrounded by fools, and he has trouble understanding how God tolerates them. He sees ignorance and injustice, and it troubles him. But because he understands prayer as communion with God, he does not try to solve these questions himself. Nor does he demand answers from God. He is content to simply share his ponderings and offers them as his prayer.

In pondering prayer we also can present our questions, wonderings and concerns to God. We do so not as a student

might ask a question of a teacher but more as you might share
with a friend with whom you have talked often about the matter. Good friends know better than to try to answer ponderings that are presented as questions. They know that you are
simply asking that they listen and hold your concerns with
you in friendship.

Psalm 15 is another pondering prayer. It begins: "Yahweh,
who can find a home in your tent, who can dwell on your holy
mountain?" The pray-er then goes on to answer his own question by describing the one whose way of life is blameless. Psalm
19 begins with the psalmist pondering the magnificence of creation while Psalm 49 is a meditation on the futility of riches
and Psalm 90 a reflection on the human condition. But what
makes these prayers? And what makes them worthy enough
example of prayer to be included in Scriptures? The answer is
the simple fact that they so clearly demonstrate the importance
of conducting our reflection on experience with awareness that
we are in the presence of God. Pondering prayer is offering that
reflection as part of our self as we open our minds and hearts
to God.

We offer a pondering prayer whenever we reflectively listen
to a sermon, a conversation or a lecture. If our minds are open
to God—once again remembering that this is part of what it
means to be taking on the mind of Christ—such reflection is
prayer. Of course this can also include reflective engagement
with a book. This present moment as you read this page can be
a prayer if it involves trusting openness before God. If it does,
your reading is an opportunity to meet God. Such reflective
engagement is not limited to devotional books. Think of the
way a good novel can immerse you in experiences and perspectives that will often leave you pondering—consciously and

unconsciously—long after you have set the book down. Make this a prayer by offering these ponderings to God. Or think of how a work of nonfiction can engage you with important issues in the world. Sharing these ponderings with God, in worded or unworded ways, is prayer.

Studying or meditating on Scriptures can also be prayer. Often this is described as discursive meditation to distinguish it from contemplative meditation. Discursive meditation is a thinking-oriented approach to meditation. When we meditate in this way we think about the passage, viewing it from many angles. We might first attempt to understand who wrote it and why. We might also try to understand who the intended audience was and what the purpose was for the writing. Once again, this sort of study is not automatically prayer because we can study Scriptures without openness of spirit. But when meditation and reflection is conducted with openness to God, this too is prayer.

Meditating on or reciting the creeds can also be a rich expression of pondering prayer. You may already be a part of a church that sings or recites one of the creeds each service. But if public use of the creeds is not part of the practice of your spiritual community, consider making it a personal practice. Take one of the major creedal statements—the Apostles' Creed, the Nicene Creed or the Athanasian Creed—and make it a focus for meditation. Or take the Lord's Prayer and use it in the same way. Prayers from a prayer book can also be used for this sort of reflection. Ponder the words. Research and reflect on the meaning. And share your ruminations with God.

Several years ago I found myself thinking about the Lord's Prayer and, beginning to discover its depths and riches, decided to make it a focus of meditation. I quickly noticed how much trouble I had making it my own. While I sang it every Sunday as part of the liturgy, I was not really making it my prayer. When I did, I noticed that I often balked at asking that God's will be done on earth as I realized that I wasn't prepared to embrace God's will in my own little corner of earth—my own life. But even more, I noticed how reluctant I was to ask that I would be forgiven by God as I forgave others. I felt God inviting me to stick with this prayer until the Lord's Prayer became my prayer, and to make it my primary form of verbal prayer until it did. I asked that through it Jesus would lead me to the one that he, praying with me, called "Our Father." And as I meditated on this prayer and offered those meditations as prayer, that began to happen. Through a period of prayerful pondering, Jesus led me into a deeper knowing of our Father, and in the process, his prayer became mine.

Take a moment of pondering prayer right now. Think about my suggestion that offering your ponderings to God can be prayer. Reflect on the possibilities this form of prayer might hold for you, and share your thoughts with God. Share also any questions you may have about it, and any desires or movements in your heart that you have noticed while reading the previous pages. And when you have done so, return to the book and pick up at this point.

JOURNALING AND THEOLOGICAL REFLECTION

Pondering requires space, not so much external physical space as internal psychological and spiritual space. It requires freedom from distractions. And because it is an inefficient form of thought that can't be rushed, it also requires time.

Journaling can be a wonderful way to create the sort of space for reflection on life experiences that is involved in pondering prayer. Of course, you can journal for many different reasons. But when a journal is used as a framework for prayer, the focus is primarily on process, not content. An exhaustive and accurate report of whatever you have experienced is not the issue. Prayerful reflection on the experience is what counts. Anything you write is simply in support of this end.

One way of thinking about what you write in this sort of journaling is to view it as a conversation with God. I know many people who write these reflections as letters to God, and they find this a tremendously meaningful form of prayer. I have done so myself. But this is not the only way to make journaling a prayer experience, because prayerful pondering is more than a conversation. Don't reduce it to communicating information or requests to God. It is better viewed as a space to hold your ruminations on your experience and to share those reflections with God. It starts with willingness to take a closer look at daily experience. Sometimes this takes courage because these experiences might involve things we would prefer to avoid. Reflection on any experience involves a degree of reexperiencing. And if the emotions that are involved in the original experience were negative, we often naturally try to minimize reexposure to them.

But reflection involves more than review. It creates space for reinterpretation of the meaning of the experience. Humans are meaning-making creatures. As soon as we experience something, we automatically set to work to weave that experience within the narrative that we are writing as our story. In other words, we assign it a meaning. For example, if I feel that a friend is suddenly being unusually slow to return my phone calls or to respond to my emails, I will inevitably assign this some meaning. I might assume that my friend is busy and think no more

about the matter. Or I may take it personally and wonder if I
have offended him. Or I may respond with irritation and assume that he no longer values my friendship. And, of course,
there are many other ways I might interpret this. But we cannot
avoid interpreting experience.

Prayerful reflection on experience offers us a chance to review the interpretation of the experience in the light of our relationship with God and our Christian community and tradition. We might speak of this as an exercise of theological
reflection. This is not something that is only suitable for those
with theological training, although there certainly is a learning
curve involved in learning to pray in this or any other new way.
But theological reflection is not thinking about theology. It is
the prayerful act of seeking meaning in experience that relies
on the rich heritage of Christian Scriptures and tradition as a
primary interpretative framework. Quite sophisticated frame-
works exist for doing this, but in its simplest form, the process
does not need to be complicated or overly elaborate.[1] It is simply examining our experience through the lens of our faith.
Described in this way you will immediately see its similarity to
the examen described in chapter four. However, while the examen is primarily a prayer of attention, the sort of theological
reflection I am describing is a prayer of pondering, in that it
gives much more room for reflective thinking.

To illustrate this, let me return to my experience of feeling
that a friend had been ignoring me. To begin I would need to
review the experience and focus on the feelings and sensations
that are now associated with it. Let's say that I feel hurt and
angry. Then, I would notice the meaning I attach to this. Doing
so I might discover that I feel betrayed; I may be interpreting
the delayed response as a personal slight. Now I am ready to

place this in a larger faith context. I might, for example, reflect on how Christ responded to those who betrayed him. That has some immediately obvious implications! I might also think about Christ's teaching about turning the other cheek—implying, in part, not being overly invested in the petty things we feel people can take from us by intended or nonintended slights. I might also recall Jesus' teaching on forgiveness, and although I am not sure if anything has been done to actually warrant forgiveness, I might notice my heart beginning to soften. None of this is cutting-edge theology. But that is not the point. The point is simply to connect my experience to my faith and my faith tradition, and allow it to shape the interpretation I give it and the way I respond to it.

Don't get lost in the details of any of this. The purpose of making space for reflection is to connect our pondering to our faith and to do so in openness to God. When we do so, it is prayer, regardless of how we may actually do it.

PRAYER AND PROBLEM SOLVING

I have a good friend who, although he is a Christian, is critical of spirituality of any sort because he views it as too anti-intellectual. He feels that the most important problems that confront humans—problems such as poverty and resource scarcity, war and terrorism, destruction of natural habitats and climate change, accumulating toxic waste, and nuclear security—demand careful analysis and good judgment. From his perspective spirituality tends to attract the soft-headed and tender-hearted. Too often, he argues, it fails to encourage careful thinking and make this a part of spiritual practice. If prayer is to support a response to these critical global issues, it must, in his view, embrace cognition and allow it to be as central to spirituality as it is to being human. I think he makes a very important point.

Spirituality has often made more room for intuition than reason. Too often it has implied that the spiritual response in any given situation is simply one of surrender and trust, suggesting that reliance on our own critical problem-solving skills is a clear indication of the absence of such trust. Often it has explicitly taught that prayer is turning problems over to God, but failed to point out that it should also include working toward their solution in divine presence and with divine assistance.

Coming to God in trusting openness does not mean abandoning our agency and responsibility. Genesis tells us that God invested in Adam and Eve responsibility for all of creation, and at no time since then is there any reason to believe that God has said: "Since you have made such a mess of things I now absolve you of that responsibility and ask that you simply trust me to take care of things." Prayer is divine communion that enables us to engage the world with renewed focus, competence and passion—and with all of our natural gifts and abilities. And pondering problems, both personal and communal, can form a central part of that experience of communion with God.

As a parent I am always pleased when our adult son consults my wife or me about decisions and issues he is facing. Last night he phoned to tell us that he was considering buying a home. He wasn't seeking advice. He called to talk through the decisions he was facing, because he trusts us and wanted to share an important moment in his life.

Pondering prayer is much like this. In prayer I share with God what is on my mind. Often I do this while on a walk. I accept Augustine's maxim of *solvitor ambulando*—things are solved by walking.[2] Sometimes when I walk, I think of God, and sometimes I explicitly direct worded thoughts to God. But my walking prayer is in no way limited to these times when I specifically speak to God. The whole experience is prayer when I walk with openness before God. And the form that this prayer often takes is pondering prayer.

But you don't have to walk for pondering to be prayer. Trusting openness of our self to God is what makes any moment a time of prayer. It is also what makes any hour or day an hour or day of prayer. We can think through issues and try to come to a decision on our own, or we can think through those same issues and try to come to a decision in communion with God. The latter is prayer—what I am calling pondering prayer.

Take a moment to note the things that you have been pondering in recent days—things that you have been weighing in your mind and carrying in your heart. Name them before God, asking God to be part of your rumination as you continue to chew on these matters. Just typing this, I quickly can identify three or four things that I know have been very much in my mind in the last couple of days but which I haven't yet invited God to share. I suspect this is true for you as well. Just naming them connects us to God as we declare our desire to open and share our heart and mind. Just being mindful of God's presence and care for all parts of our experience is integrating, because it reminds us that there is no part of us or of our experience God is not interested in.

MIND AND HEART

While pondering often begins with thoughts, if pursued it can move us beyond the mind to the heart. Pondering pays attention to both thoughts and feelings. The two are always closely

linked. Pondering allows us to follow the currents of either as
they flow out in ripples that inevitably include the other. Of
course, some people tend to remain stuck in either thoughts or
feelings, and spend little time attending to the other. But prayer
invites us to ponder the movements of both mind and heart,
and share these with God.

I mentioned in a previous chapter that Mary, the mother of
Jesus, knew how to make both mind and heart part of her life
of prayer. When she was told by the angel that she had been
chosen to bear the Christ child, not surprisingly her first response to the news was to be troubled. Noticing this, the angel
told her not to fear, reminding her that she had already won
God's favor. But quickly, ripples of this initial opening movement of the heart reached her head. Now she began thinking
through the implications of what she heard. Suddenly she was
puzzled, and she responded to this bewilderment by asking the
angel an extremely practical and important question: "But how
can this come about, since I have no knowledge of man?" (Luke
1:34). The expression of both her troubled heart and her troubled mind were prayer because they were shared in trusting
openness with God.

In the chapter immediately following this story we encounter the record of the birth of Jesus and the visit of the shepherds. Here also we see how closely aligned Mary's head and
heart were, and how easily she opened both to God. Luke notes
that, hearing the shepherds describe to her and the others what
the angels had told them about the Christ child, the others were
astonished at what they heard. Mary, he said, responded by
pondering these things in her heart (Luke 2:19). Surely she was
still filled with questions. And undoubtedly she also experienced an astounding range of emotions. She did not ignore any

of this. Instead she pondered the totality of her experience as she opened both her head and heart to God.

Pondering is not, therefore, simply a mental activity. It will usually be thought-based, but it will never exclude the emotions. Mind and heart should both be opened to God in prayer if that prayer is to link us in our depths and totality with God. Pondering involves thinking, but it also involves paying attention to where that thinking leads me. It includes, therefore, paying attention to the way the process impacts my heart or my deeper self.

During the last several months I have been thinking through a decision. A friend asked me to serve as a mentor for students in a new Ph.D. program he was developing. In order to answer whether or not I would do this, I first had to think through what I hoped it might achieve and what I anticipated it would involve. I did much of this thinking with God. In the same way, I also shared my thoughts with my wife. In both cases I opened my self and my thought processes to people I trusted and whose communion I enjoyed.

There was, however, another component of my pondering, and this turned out to be a critical one. I also pondered in my heart. I paid attention not just to mental contents and processes but also to the movements within my spirit. I noted, for example, that I often felt troubled as I was thinking through the issues involved in this mentoring experience. I could have simply judged this to be a distracting irrelevance and tried to ignore it, but pondering demands attention not just to the content issues that appear in the mind but also to the process ones that register on the heart.

And so, noting these, I discussed them with God. I wondered with God what this cloud on my spirit represented and what implications it suggested. If I was honest, I was irritated at its presence. I wanted to accept the invitation and was excited about undertaking the challenge. But the cloud hanging over my spirit did not lift—at least not until I finally discerned what it was that was bothering me. Prayerfully attending to my heart helped me discern my disquiet. I wanted to do what I was being asked to consider so badly that I was ignoring the fact that I did not really think that this mentoring experience could do what I or the institution hoped it would do—at least within the parameters of what was possible.

Attending to that heart data was not a distraction. Ultimately, it allowed me to make the best decision. I arrived at that decision through pondering prayer. Certainly I prayed that God would help me to know what to do. But more than this, as I pondered the whole matter in God's presence slowly it become more and more clear that I should decline the invitation.

In prayer we bring heart and mind in openness to God. Pondering allows us to drill down into an issue with focused rational analysis and critical thinking, but it also allows us to step back from this drilling and attend to other data that does not register on the mind but in the heart. Pondering as prayer involves sharing all or any of this with God, who longs that we come and share our experience and enjoy the communion that is prayer.

PRAYING WITH IMAGINATION

But pondering involves even more than reflection on our experience and the thoughts, questions and emotions this raises. Just as the senses have an important role to play in attending prayer, so too the imagination has an important role in pondering prayer. Like the senses, the imagination has also often been mistrusted and marginalized in terms of its contribution to spiritual life. However, like the senses, the imagination can only be ignored at the expense of a rich prayer life.

Recently, after stating something like this in a talk I was giving, a woman approached me saying that she had always been taught that the imagination was unimportant, even potentially dangerous, because it was not true. I asked her if she ever read novels. She said she didn't. All she ever read, she told me, was nonfiction because this, she felt, kept her grounded in reality. She may have been well grounded, but all appearances suggested that she was far from experiencing any soaring of spirit. Fear kept her from trusting that her imagination could give her perspectives on reality that facts and reason could never provide. It also kept her spiritually impoverished. Reason has the same potential for misuse as the imagination and does not deserve, therefore, to be privileged in the way it often is. Both can be used for good and for ill, and while many of us gravitate toward one or the other, we lose something of our full humanity when we overemphasize one to the exclusion of the other.[3]

There are many ways of bringing your imagination into Christian prayer. One of the simplest is allowing it to be part of your engagement with Scripture.[4] If a passage that you are reading contains a scene or description of some action or encounter (as, for example, is common if it is drawn from the Gospels), enter this scene in your imagination. Imagine the time of day, season of the year, the sounds and smells that might be present—all the elements that would make this scene real to you. Be there in the scene with the participants. Notice your vantage point—how central or peripheral you place yourself. Consider changing your vantage point. Dare to engage the participants in an imaginary conversation. Transport yourself into the setting and open all your senses to God's presence and revelation. Allow this to become part of what you now ponder in your heart and mind. Consider the significance of what you have received, noting again what has emerged in your senses and imagination, mind and heart as you have opened yourself to God.

Take a moment to try this. Consider the following Gospel story of a moment in the life of Jesus:

> On their return the apostles gave him an account of all they had done. Then he took them with him and withdrew towards a town called Bethsaida where they could be by themselves. But the crowds got to know and they went after him. He made them welcome and talked to them about the kingdom of God; and he cured those who were in need of healing. It was late afternoon when the Twelve came up to him and said, "Send the people away, and they can go to the villages and farms round about to find lodging and food; for we are in a lonely place here." He replied, "Give them something to eat yourselves." But they said, "We have no more than five loaves and two fish, unless we are to go ourselves and buy food for all these people." For there were about five thousand men. But he said to his disciples, "Get them to sit down in parties of about fifty." They did so and made them all sit down. Then he took the five loaves and the two fish, raised his eyes to heaven, and said the blessing over them; then he broke them and handed them to his disciples to distribute among the crowd. They all ate as much as they wanted, and when the scraps left over were collected they filled twelve baskets. (Luke 9:10-17)

Ponder this story, but allow your imagination to be part of that pondering. Follow Jesus and the disciples as they travel on the road to Bethsaida, hoping for some time alone. Notice the crowds following after them. Now turn your attention back to Jesus. Notice how the disciples seem to respond to the discovery that they were followed. Observe how they react to Jesus when he welcomes the crowd and begins to cure those who were sick. And now watch as Jesus takes the five small loaves and two fish that were supposed to be the evening meal for him and the disciples, and begins to distribute it to the crowd. Look into the faces of the disciples. Listen to what they are saying to each other. Take some of the food yourself as Jesus hands you a portion. Taste it. And notice your own response as you watch the few small bits of food multiply until everyone has more than enough and there still is plenty left over. What thoughts and questions are forming in your mind? Share these with Jesus. Listen to him as he responds to you. What does he say? Ponder what it means to have received bread from the living Bread. Think about the significance of the event you have witnessed and share your thoughts with Jesus.

Being imaginatively present to Jesus in the events of his life recorded in Scripture can be a tremendously enriching part of pondering prayer. It makes the encounter personal and present—something happening in the present moment. Perhaps you felt too awkward to engage Jesus in imaginative conversation. That's fine. Just go as far with this exercise as you wish. However, if you were able to do this I suspect that, like the first time I did so, you might have been quite surprised by how immediate and intimate the encounter was. Spirit-guided imaginative engagement in prayer simply brings yet other parts of our self into the prayer experience and opens up even more dimensions of our being to God.

Another way to do this is to meditate on Christian religious art.[5] This offers us a wonderfully rich resource for prayerful pondering. Thousands of great works of art have been produced as meditations on passages of Scripture. Sitting before them and meditatively gazing on them is engaging the senses and the imagination in a conversation with God. Using the artist's meditation as a springboard for your own helps you engage with the Word behind the words of Scripture. And it does so by involving the senses and the imagination.

CULTIVATING PRAYERFUL PONDERING

Pondering prayer is responding to the invitation to bring your mind, heart and imagination to your communion with God. Let me suggest several practical things you can do if you wish to further cultivate this sort of prayer.

1. Begin by including a brief time of sharing the things you have been thinking about in any time of worded prayer. Talk with God about the things that have been heavy on your heart or mind. Even simply naming them is prayer. For example, you might say: "Lord, you know I have been thinking a lot these days about my finances. I offer you that thinking." Or "Lord, I am concerned about my mother's health and unsure whether to advise her to undergo further chemotherapy. I offer you my thinking and concerns." As you prepare yourself for prayer by gathering yourself in stillness, simply make your first words a naming of your present realities—

including the things you have been pondering in heart and mind. For most of us it takes no special effort to remember to make time to ponder things. We do so naturally much of our waking hours, and this pondering then carries over into our sleep, often translating itself into the content of our dreams. What we need to remember is to share these ponderings with God. This invites God to be a part of our inner life and gives God access to our depths.

2. Ponder the meaning and significance of some of the major Christian rituals and practices that are part of your life. Think through, for example, what prayer means to you—not just how you understand it or what it should mean, but its actual significance to you. Ponder the meaning and personal significance of Communion (or the Eucharist) the next time you receive it. Listen carefully to the words that are spoken in the preparation for this moment and in the distribution of the elements. Ponder them during and after the experience. Do the same with other regular elements of your own church tradition. Next time you witness a baptism, think again of the significance of your own baptism and of the baptismal vows taken by you or offered on your behalf by others. Take some of these familiar elements of religious practice and open them up for deeper personal meaning as you engage with them in pondering prayer.

3. The next time you find yourself reflecting on some recent personal experience, take a moment to invite

God to be part of this process. Remember, bidden or not, God is already present. And anything that is on your heart and in your mind is an issue of importance to God. Start by focusing on the experience. This grounds the reflection and makes it quite different from abstract speculation. After reviewing the experience for a few moments, step back from the details of what happened and view the whole situation through the lens of your faith and your faith tradition. What images form in your mind as you think about the experience? Do any of these images seem to point toward God? What are the main issues and values that are embedded in the situation? Do any Scripture stories of biblical or theological images come to mind in relation to them? If so, how do they either affirm or challenge the meaning and understanding you were developing of the incident? Does the situation involve any important Christian ethical issues— sexism, class relations, justice, morality, racism, power or resource distribution? How might Jesus respond to the situation, or how did he face a similar one that was recorded in Scriptures? How do theological themes of sin, suffering, evil, grace, salvation or others that are prominent in your own tradition relate to the situation and affect your understanding of it? These questions are one way of making space for theological reflection on experience. Doing so is pondering prayer.

4. Watch for an opportunity to make God a part of your pondering of the larger social and global issues that are of greatest concern to you at the moment. The next time

you read or think about these big issues, do so through the framework of your faith and make your reflection on them one of pondering prayer. Ask again the questions suggested in the previous paragraph as a way of bringing theological reflection to bear on these issues. And don't forget to engage your best critical thinking as you seek prayerfully to understand and be guided in your response to them. This too is prayer.

5. Finally, be imaginative in your pondering. This means taking care that you don't become bogged down in the ruts of rumination that can sometimes form when you ponder something over a long period of time. Allow your pondering to be creative, expansive and generative. Genuinely view whatever you ponder from different angles. This is what you were doing in bringing theological reflection to bear on the issue. Now broaden the boundaries of your reflection even more as you invite God to help you see the issues from a divine and eternal perspective. Imaginative pondering is not just allowing images to form in your mind. It is also allowing yourself to adopt alternate and multiple perspectives on the issues. Be attentive to such alternate perspectives in what you read and as you listen to others talk about the issues of concern. Don't simply dismiss their point of view. Try it on for size as you seek to discover and bring the mind of Christ to the issues.

PRAYER AS RESPONDING

IN PRAYER, AS IN LIFE, IT IS POSSIBLE to become stuck in awareness and pondering, and fail to respond with action. Notice your patterns of procrastination. Like mine, they probably involve things that you think about and are aware are important, but choose to do nothing about—at least not yet. Exercise and other lifestyle changes come quickly to mind for me, but your list may differ. Similar blocks can also exist in prayer.

The complete prayer process is truncated if attending and pondering never lead to a response. Not every action of attention or pondering demands a response, but if none do, we are stuck in a place of incomplete prayer. There are as many ways we can respond as there are people. This is part of our uniqueness. No single response is suitable for all. But some response is essential if we are to be open to God with the totality of our being.

PRAYING WITH WORDS

At last we get to what most people think of prayer! Worded prayer—either audible or silent—will usually form the majority of what we consciously offer as intentional acts of prayer.

We now know that it is far from all that is included in prayer, but it is quite appropriate to think of it as the main form of prayer.

When asked by his disciples to teach them how to pray, Jesus taught worded prayer. While he certainly taught other forms of prayer by example, what Protestant's typically call the "Lord's Prayer" and Roman Catholics call the "Our Father" is a worded prayer suitable for either audible or silent use by either individuals or groups. Nor surprisingly, therefore, it has often been analyzed in attempts to identify the elements of prayer that our Lord encouraged. Before we consider those, let us remind ourselves of the prayer.

Our Father who art in heaven,
Hallowed be thy Name,
Thy kingdom come, Thy will be done,
    on earth as it is in heaven.
Give us this day our daily bread;
And forgive us our trespasses,
    As we forgive them that trespass against us;
And lead us not into temptation, But deliver us from evil.
For thine is the kingdom, the power, and the glory,
        For ever and ever. Amen.[1]

It is possible to classify the components of this prayer—and therefore the dimensions of worded prayer—in quite a number of different ways. Let me suggest a simple classification built around four elements.

1. *Faith*. Prayer is an expression of trust, and trust is the essential core of faith. A complete worded prayer always, therefore, includes some expression of our faith. In this model prayer of Jesus, faith is expressed by the opening phrase, "Our

Father." In faith we dare address our divine Parent, and in faith we name God as ours. We pray to the one Jesus called his Father because in faith we accept that in Christ we share his Father as ours. We can invoke God as our divine Parent because the Son has revealed him as such to us. In the Son, through our baptism, we are adopted as daughters and sons of this God we address as ours.

2. Praise. Describing God as being "in heaven" is an expression of praise. This does not refer to a spatial location but rather to a way of being. It affirms that God is majestic. It also suggests that God is transcendent and holy—unimaginably beyond anything we can imagine. This theme is echoed in the next phrase, "Hallowed be thy Name." In this we affirm that God is holy and express our desire that the entire world would recognize the presence of God and respond with awe and reverence.

3. Kingdom hope. This is followed by several expressions of our hope in the kingdom of God—a hope in God's reign that has begun on earth but has yet to come to fulfillment. First we pray, "Thy kingdom come." What this means is made more clear in the next expression, "Thy will be done, on earth as it is in heaven." We ask that God's reign on earth would be as it is in heaven, this being seen in the fulfillment of God's perfect will. This fulfillment is and will be the kingdom of God.

4. Petitions and intercession. This is followed by an even more explicit series of petitions, reminding us that asking for things from God is an important part of prayer. We first ask for our daily bread, representing our needs. In making this prayer mine, I ask along with all those who turn to God in faith, and in so doing I acknowledge that this bread is not mine but ours. It comes with a responsibility to share. I do not, therefore, ask only for myself. I request that which I need but which I can then pass on to others, thus reflecting the loving heart of the God whom I petition. This reminds us of the important role of intercession—praying for and on behalf of others. For many people intercession forms the core of their prayer life. While holistic prayer should not be limited to this, calling on God to be merciful to those we hold in our hearts in love is without question an important part of Christian prayer.

We then ask for forgiveness. This is only appropriate since we have acknowledged the holiness of God, and in so doing are reminded of our own lack. However, the next phrase is perhaps more surprising. We ask that our trespasses be forgiven in the same manner we have forgiven those who trespassed against us. Once again, therefore, this prayer reminds us of our responsibility—first to share our daily bread and then to forgive as we desire that God may forgive us.

Finally, the prayer concludes with a request that we not be led into temptation but delivered from evil. We ask for help to be able to resist temptation and be protected from the evil one. But it is also a request that we be delivered from all evils—past, present and future. It is a request, therefore, that we be kept in and protected by the holiness of God. And so, with this, we return to an expression of praise for the majestic One who resides in heaven, beyond evil and full of eternal power and glory.

Although there is value in identifying elements of worded prayer, I do not believe that every worded prayer must contain all these components. To interpret the Lord's Prayer in such a literal way is to treat it too legalistically. Sometimes when our prayer response leads us to worded communication with God, what we will need to express is just one of these dimensions. At other times what we need to express will not seem to be represented in this model prayer. This does not mean that it is not appropriate. Think, for example, of Jesus' prayers of agony in the garden of Gethsemane. Just because the Lord's Prayer does not contain a corresponding expression of agony does not mean that something like "My God, my God, why have you forsaken me?" (Matthew 27:46) is not an appropriate verbal prayer. Or just because it does not contain an expression of thanksgiving does not mean that communicating gratitude is inappropriate. Obviously gratitude is an important part of prayer, as is lament. Prayer is turning in trust and opening our self to God—sharing whatever is within our self.

However, over time, worded prayer will usually move across these various elements. The words we use will usually fit somewhere within these big categories of expressions of our faith, praise, hopes and petitions. But remember that prayer is not so much what we do as what God does in us. It is not our job to offer perfect prayers that follow some kind of a formula. Our job is to open our self to God and allow our self to respond to our experience. And often that response will require words.

Worded prayers may, of course, be composed by our self and offered extemporaneously, or they may be our offering of a prayer written by someone else. Unfortunately, some churches value one of these and despise the other, or are only comfortable with one and avoid the other. But both types of prayer have immense value.

We have already identified the value of simple worded expressions of our own heart and mind. Sometimes this is called conversational prayer. Often it is thought of as personal prayer. But liturgical prayers that have been written by others can be equally personal when they are offered as our own, regardless of whether we are praying the prayer on our own in private devotion or as part of a community of worshipers. Prayer is personal. There is no such thing as impersonal prayer. There can be impersonal statements of theology, but prayer is always an expression of a heart and mind that is open to God in trust, responding to the movement of God in one's self.

Worded prayer is where most of us begin our prayer journey. But while it is an excellent beginning point, if prayer does not move beyond words it will gradually dry up and prove tiresome and frustrating. The problem is not simply the limitations of words, but is also the limited parts of our self that are involved in communion with the divine if our encounter is restricted to words. God invites not just our cognitive self but our whole self. Consequently, learning to involve other parts of our self in our prayer response is important if we are to allow God to move in and through our total self and if prayer is to emerge as a response of that total self.

PRAYING WITH MUSIC

Music is a powerful means of engaging some of the other parts of our self that are invited to the divine encounter. This is why singing is so central to Christian worship. Simply adding music to words means that more of our self is now involved in the experience. No longer is prayer simply an expression of thoughts. Music engages our emotions and the body as well as other deep parts of our self that are excluded from an encounter that is based exclusively on thoughts. It also evokes memories and brings us back in touch with important experiences. It is therefore an important resource in moving toward prayer as an opening of the total self to God.

I know many people whose most meaningful prayer response involves singing, playing or listening to music that expresses words that they make their own. Curiously, some of these people come from church traditions that belittle offering worded prayers that have been written by others. But what makes these prayers acceptable is that they are carried from their heart to the heart of God by music. This is, of course, a wonderful illustration of prayer as response. Those who pray with music in this way recognize that prayer is not simply what they do but allowing what God places in their heart to return to God. And they are absolutely correct in that deep knowing—whether they have ever expressed it in those terms or not.

Music can, however, also carry the spirit heavenward as a response to the Spirit that does not involve words that are understood or does not involve words at all. Some of the music that carries my deepest prayer response is choral music composed and sung in languages of which I know only, at best, a small number of words. Few things, for example, stir my spirit and express my deepest prayer like the forty-voice medieval motet *Spem in Alium* by Thomas Tallis. The fact that it is sung in Latin does not detract from my prayer experience but rather enhances it. Because I do not understand most of the words, the left hemisphere of my cerebral cortex can enjoy a welcome rest as the deeper places of my spirit and soul soar toward God. This is the same thing that happens for me when I listen to jazz. But it may be rock, contemporary Christian, classical, world or some quite different musical genre that carries your deepest prayers. In each case, music is the medium through which the Spirit of God touches us in the deep places of our individuality and invites us to respond by allowing that music to be the vehicle of communion with God. And for those with musical talent, making music can, of course, also be a wonderfully creative and rich prayer response.

Take a pause from reading to pray with music right now. Listen to whatever music you select—setting everything else aside and really engaging with it. Open yourself to this music, and through it, to God. Or make the music yourself and allow it to creatively flow from your depths. Respond to the invitations of the Spirit that turn your heart and spirit toward God.

PRAYING WITH CREATIVITY

But music is not the only way we can offer an artistic or creative prayer response. The response that bursts forth from within you may be to write a poem, paint a picture, create or perform a piece of music, or dance, but it may also be to prepare a meal, face a conflict you have been avoiding or simply and truly be yourself with a friend, or in some more public way.

Creativity, like thought, is undoubtedly also one of the important ways humans show divine likeness. God creates, and we are made in God's image. Consequently, creativity springs forth from all of us, in one way or another. We do not always trust its voice, and when distracted we may not even discern its presence. We tend to think of creativity only in certain limited spheres of life—the arts, for example—and fail to see that any act that emerges with authenticity from a deep place of spirit and soul is a creative one.

As part of the research for another book I am presently writing I recently asked a number of people to describe the circumstances in which they feel most at one and at peace within themselves.[2] Their answers were diverse and fascinating. Many spoke about times with someone they loved. Others described the stillness of being in solitude. Some spoke of times of preparing meals or caring for children. However, when I asked them what was most satisfying about these experiences, one answer emerged over and over again. They told me that these were situations in which they experienced themselves as being true to their self in some deep way. Being our true self is an act of being that always involves creativity and originality, and it is prayer when it is offered in openness and trust to God.

Of course we recognize the great artists among us as expressing creativity, and perhaps we can, consequently, see how artistic expressions can be a prayer of creative response. But in order to see more clearly how all of us possess the possibilities of creative prayerful response, let me briefly share the story of one of the people I interviewed.

Gordon was eighty-six years old when we talked.[3] Recently remarried after a protracted period of grief following the death of his wife of fifty-one years, he had once again embraced life and was living with the zest and passion that had long characterized him. Living on a lake in a remote part of northern Minnesota, he said he felt at home in a way he had never been in the urban settings that had been the context of his earlier life. Here, during the summer months, he paddled his new bride around the lake in his canoe, and during the winter he walked to town with snowshoes to get food and other supplies. He also took up horseback riding—something he said he had always wanted to do but never had the opportunity. Riding soon led to jumping, although he had recently been persuaded to give this up when he fell off his horse while jumping over a fence! His life was joyfully full, and it overflowed in love to all he encountered. He spent hours each week working as a volunteer at a drop-in center for young people in the nearby small town, and his home was filled with people who were drawn to him because of the vitality that sprang from the depths of his being and contagiously drew them into a more passionate engagement with life.

I asked Gordon how he understood the gift of his life. He spoke of his family and the joy of his new marriage. But he also talked about having learned to be free to be himself. He said he had discovered that there was a simple and natural way of being in the world and with God, and that this was who he was called to be. Each of us is similarly called to be the unique and original self that we are in God.[4] Doing so is praying with creativity.

PRAYING WITH HANDS AND FEET

Prayer is, as I suggested in chapter one, so much more than what we usually think or realize. Not only can we pray with words. We can even pray with our hands and with our feet! I am presently praying with my fingers as I write this chapter. Journaling is, of course, another form of praying with your hands. There are, however, several even more ancient prayer traditions that have played an important role in Christian spirituality over the millennia.

One of the earliest ways of praying by hand was signing the cross. Well established by the second century, pray-ers would trace the sign of the cross on their body or in the air, often while repeating the trinitarian formula "In the name of the Father, and the Son, and the Holy Spirit." With slight differences in the way this is done in Eastern Orthodox churches and Western churches (Roman Catholic, Anglican/Episcopal, Lutheran and some Methodist), this prayer of the hand is for millions of Christians a symbolic invocation of the trinitarian God. Nothing needs to be said for this prayer to be offered. All it takes is making the sign of the cross.

While nonliturgical Christians tend to not cross themselves, they often wear crosses, which have the potential to serve the same purpose. In order to help keep the meaning of the cross in mind, the one I wear beneath my shirt is purposefully rather heavy, its movement in response to my movements giving me frequent cause to remember that I carry the cross of Christ on my body. However, worn crosses are easily forgotten and often function simply as jewelry, whereas the intentionality of signing the cross tends to make this a more conscious prayer. But once again we are reminded that there is no single correct way to pray—even to remain mindfully connected to the central symbol of the Christian faith, the cross.

Another early Christian practice of praying with hands was first seen in the second- and third-century desert monks, who used stones as an aid to prayer. Sitting on the ground the pray-er would have a heap of stones that had been collected and counted, and would move these, one at a time, after each repetition of the Jesus Prayer—"Lord Jesus Christ, Son of God, have mercy upon me, a sinner."[5] The stones served to keep the pray-er in place, freeing the spirit even as it engaged the body. They also served as a way of keeping track of the number of repetitions—this often being 150 (for the number of psalms in the Psalter). By the fourth century the repetition of the Jesus Prayer was a standard feature of monastic prayer. Basil the Great recommended, however, that stones be replaced by the use of a knotted or beaded cord.[6] Prayers that are structured by this cord—called a "chotki"—continue to be central to the life of Eastern Orthodox Christians to this day.

The best known Roman Catholic prayer with beads is the rosary. This is a circle of beads that guides the pray-er through repeated sequences of a cycle of prayers.[7] Each cycle is followed by a meditation on one of the events in the life of Jesus Christ or his mother, the Blessed Virgin Mary. This popular devotional form of prayer is much more than a prayer of words. Through repetition aided by the elements of touch and movement, it gradually sinks from consciousness to the unconscious. It is, therefore, a deep and extremely important prayer form that has, as its most visible manifestation, the movement of beads through one's fingers.

Adaptations of these Eastern Orthodox and Roman Catholic ways of praying with beads can be found in a number of other Christian traditions. In Norway I encountered a Lutheran version that involves eighteen beads of different shapes and textures, which are used to guide the pray-er through a series of meditations. Called the "Pearls of Life" (or sometimes the "Wreath of Christ"), they are often worn as a bracelet, the pray-er fingering each of the nine different types of beads and silently offering the short prayer that is associated with each. Another recent adaptation is the Anglican prayer beads, where thirty-three beads (corresponding to the thirty-three years of our Lord's life) are divided into groups, with an initiatory cruciform bead that begins the prayer sequence. Regardless of these various denominational names, Christians of many traditions make use of these and other prayer beads, and in so doing move their prayer from their heads to deep places within body, spirit and soul.

Praying with our feet works in much the same way as praying with our hands. Once again, the elements of touch and movement help keep our mind from wandering, and the rhythm of the prayer helps bring body, mind and spirit into the presence of God. Walking prayer can be a prayer of attentiveness, pondering, response or contemplation. I have already mentioned it in earlier chapters, so here let me say something about walking as response. In chapter seven we will consider its role in contemplative prayer.

Choosing to walk as a response and way of being present to God involves more than simply trying to remember to talk to God when you happen to be walking. Here, the response that I might feel impelled to make to the movement of the Spirit within my spirit is to walk. Pilgrimage is a good example of this. Christian pilgrimage is rooted in the pilgrimages the Jews historically made to Jerusalem. The so-called Psalms of Ascents—Psalms 120–134—were the songs sung by pilgrims on these journeys. Jews call these psalms *Maʾalot*, meaning "steps" or "ascent"—referring to the ascent to Jerusalem that ended with the ascent of the steps of the temple. In synagogues and churches around the world these psalms are still being recited even though many of us have lost touch with their original context and fail to recall the spiritual value of pilgrimage.

At the core of pilgrimage is a journey. But unlike most journeys, travel is not simply a means of getting to a destination. The pilgrim's journey is both means and end. Often a destination is chosen because of its spiritual significance. At the end of the very popular Santiago de Compostela pilgrimage in northern Spain is a cathedral where tradition has it that the remains of the apostle James are buried. Among many other destinations, Christians have also long made pilgrimages to Jerusalem (because of its significance in the life of Christ and its importance to understanding the Psalms of Ascents) and Lourdes (because of its longstanding reputation as a place of miraculous healing). However, pilgrims quickly come to appreciate that the journey is itself transformational when it is undertaken with prayerful openness to God. The longing behind the actions makes pilgrimage prayer. When this longing points toward God, our heart and spirit are pointed toward God, and our feet are simply following the urgings of Spirit as we are moved to prayer.

Pilgrimage always involves both an exterior and interior journey. Any travel can be a pilgrimage, regardless of the destination or whether or not there even is a destination. The difference between a pilgrim and a tourist is the intention of *attention* and *openness* to God. This transforms a trip into a pilgrimage, and the result is that the self that sets out on pilgrimage will not be the same as the self that returns. When travel is undertaken with longings that point toward God, the journey will be sacred because it is an act of transformational prayer.

We cannot all make a pilgrimage to Santiago de Compostela, Jerusalem or Lourdes. Nor can some people travel anywhere. So, over the centuries symbolic ways of making pilgrimage have been developed. The best known of these is walking a labyrinth or even tracing one on the palm of our hand. Unlike mazes, which are filled with dead ends and complicated patterns, labyrinths are created for prayer rather than designed as puzzles. In a labyrinth a single path leads through many turns, but when followed to its end it inevitably brings us to the center. Then, when we are ready, it leads us out again. Irene Alexander describes the wonderful implication of this: "If I keep walking the spiritual journey, if I trust myself to the journey, and to the Divine Other, I must at last come to the Center. My task is to trust and to continue to journey."[8]

Labyrinths can be readily found in retreat centers and cathedrals around the world. Apart from walking them in prayerful openness to God, there is no one correct way to offer this prayer. In my own practice I make a point of bringing with me anything that troubles me or any questions that I am carrying in my heart. As I approach the center—which, as on the path of life seems closer at times and farther away at others (it can, however, always be seen)—my anticipation of resting in the presence of God heightens. When I arrive there, I leave with God whatever things I have been carrying. I stay at the center for as long as I wish, enjoying God's presence. And then I gently return to my everyday world, taking with me a renewed sense of union with God and gratitude for any other gifts I have received.

I try to walk labyrinths wherever I encounter them. They are a very important prayer form for me because they don't involve words. I am a person of words. I have spent most of my life thinking, speaking and writing. Prayer that does not involve words is, therefore, tremendously freeing and healing for me. It lets me step out of the word-centered ruts of my life and allows me to enact my engagement with God in a bodily way. When I then return to my world of words, I bring my body back with me. This is why labyrinth prayer is so healing for me. As we dare to bring more and more of us to the encounter with God, we are made more whole.

PRAYING WITH LOVING SERVICE

Recently I had a conversation with a friend who works as the manager of a residential treatment program for drug addicts. I know that she does not consider herself to be religious or even spiritual. She has told me that she seldom prays and that she maintains her Quaker connections more because of the values of the community than as a way of connecting to God. Her connection to God, she says, occurs primarily in and through her work. So this time when we were together I asked her to tell me what kept her going in this work and how it connected her to God. As

I listened to her speak of the people in her program and her strong desire to make a difference in their lives, I was deeply touched by her compassion and commitment to the people she served, not simply to a job. She told me that she felt she was serving God and that this was why her work felt so sacred.

This woman was indeed a woman of prayer. In case that seems to stretch prayer too much, listen to the words of Jesus (Matthew 25:31-40):

> When the Son of man comes in his glory, escorted by all the angels, then he will take his seat on his throne of glory. All nations will be assembled before him and he will separate people one from another as the shepherd separates sheep from goats. He will place the sheep on his right hand and the goats on his left. Then the King will say to those on his right hand, "Come, you whom my Father has blessed, take as your heritage the kingdom prepared for you since the foundation of the world. For I was hungry and you gave me food, I was thirsty and you gave me drink, I was a stranger and you made me welcome, lacking clothes and you clothed me, sick and you visited me, in prison and you came to see me." Then the upright will say to him in reply, "Lord, when did we see you hungry and feed you, or thirsty and give you drink? When did we see you a stranger and make you welcome, lacking clothes and clothe you? When did we find you sick or in prison and go to see you?" And the King will answer, "In truth I tell you, in so far as you did this to one of the least of these brothers of mine, you did it to me."

All loving actions reveal the presence of God. Love comes from God, for God is love. *Ubi caritas et amor, Deus ibi est—*

where charity and love are, there God is. All acts of love participate in and flow from God. This is why the apostle John says, "My dear friends, let us love one another, since love is from God and everyone who loves is a child of God and knows God. . . . God is love, and whoever remains in love remains in God and God in him" (1 John 4:7, 16). God is love's origin. But so too is God love's end. Love given to others in need is love given to God. Love is always God flowing through us and back again to God. This is why the presence of genuine love is such an unequivocal indicator of the presence of God. A heart that is genuinely open to love is a heart that is genuinely open to God—whether the person recognizes this to be true or not—and this is why acts of love are acts of prayer. As with love, the origin and end of prayer is God. Our role with prayer, as with love, is to allow it to flow through us rather than block its flow.

Advocating for justice or acting in ways to bring it about can also be acts of prayer. They are so, however, when they grow out of love, not simply anger. Social action that emerges from a heart that is open to God will reflect the heart of God—a heart that always combines a passion for justice with passionate love.

CULTIVATING PRAYERFUL RESPONDING

Prayer can include not just thoughts and words but our hearts, hands, feet and even our way of living. The ways of responding that we have discussed in this chapter illustrate only a few of the many possibilities. There are, of course, as many ways of praying as there are people.

Prayer is the opening of our self to God, and each of us is a unique self. Our ways of responding to God should therefore reflect that uniqueness. Consider the following suggestions if you wish to further cultivate responding prayer as way of creatively living out your uniqueness.

1. Broaden the scope of your worded prayer. If your prayers are primarily your own personally crafted extemporaneous expressions, consult a book of prayers and see what it contributes to your encounter with God. Many such books are readily available and easily found. If, on the other hand, your worded prayers are primarily liturgical, try having a conversation with God in your own words. Review the four major components of prayer included in the model prayer offered by Jesus. Pay attention to any invitation that the Spirit may be offering you to broaden your worded prayer expressions by including any of these components that may not typically be present in your prayers. Or, if you have never before offered personally worded prayers to God, simply speak to God about where you find yourself at this point in time, and speak just as you would to a friend. There is no better place to start worded prayer.

2. Embrace the ways God meets you in your uniqueness. Where do you feel closest to God? What things represent special and important ways you can open yourself to God? Whatever these are, they can be considered means of grace. They are ways God comes to

you. Your part is to make space for these encounters with God. It may be time in your garden or with your grandchildren or a niece or nephew, or time for a contemplative walk. Whatever form it takes, these are times of prayer if they open you to God. Embrace these ways God meets you, and enter them with openness not just to the experience but to the God who is with you in them.

3. Let love flow through you. Consider the role that love plays in your prayer practice and life. As you look at the world through God's eyes (attending) and reflect on the people in your life and important issues that weigh heavily on your heart (pondering), consider how you can respond to God's love by allowing that love to flow through you more freely and fully. Prayer should never be simply a private me-and-God matter. Such a view of Christian spirituality is far too egocentric. Recall the pattern we saw in the Lord's Prayer, the Our Father. Our prayer may feel like our own, but we offer it as part of a community who address God collectively as "Our Father." In prayer we have one eye on God but the other eye keeps drifting—as it were—out to the world that God loves. God's love is intended to always move us out into that world in loving service and acts of social justice, not to merely feel the warm glow of personally received love. Open yourself to God's love, and let it flow through you.

God does not need our prayer response. We need it.

Praying in response to attending and pondering is as natural as eating in response to hunger and the presence of food. It is simply unnatural to block this natural flow. Let go, and let your body, soul and spirit respond to God. This is prayer.

PRAYER AS BEING

THE PRAYER FORMS WE HAVE considered to this point—prayer as attending, pondering and responding—are based on things we do. However, prayer is more than what we do—even more than praying. We come now to the expression of prayer that goes most beyond doing. It is prayer as being.

Allowing prayer to sink to the level of our very being is the gift of the Spirit that results from hearing, pondering and responding to God's communication. It is not as mysterious as it sounds. In essence, it is being *with* God. It is experiential knowing of our being *in* God. It is resting in the presence of the One whose word and presence have invited us into being and into relationship with the ground of our being. That word, having touched both our minds and our hearts, now leads us into quiet rest in the Beloved. And, as anyone who has ever been in love knows, words are now much less necessary. This is a prayer of shared presence, a prayer of simply being with God.

Notice that we are back again to speaking of love. This is no coincidence since God is love and we are talking about a form of prayer that involves being in the One known as love. Think of it as something like reading a love letter.[1] Imagine the experience of absence from the one you most deeply love, and then picture yourself sitting down to read a letter from him or her. You read this letter with great attentiveness as a way of drawing closer to the one whose words touch your heart. As you read, you might pause—not wanting to rush the experience. What you seek in reading the letter is not simply words or information, but contact with your beloved. And so, in addition to being attentive to the words, you also ponder the experience they evoke. The words initiate a reverie of love, and you make space for this to develop. As you savor this reverie, it is as if the one who wrote the letter suddenly walks into the room. Your heart is instantly filled with joy. You are speechless. Your embrace says everything that needs to be said as you enjoy the experience of shared presence and communion. And so it can be with God.

Usually called contemplative prayer, there is, unfortunately, a great deal of misunderstanding associated with this way of being with God in wordless communion. Sometimes it is presented in terms that are rather elitist, suggesting that all other forms of prayer are insignificant or immature. Often, teaching about it is confusing and obscure. I well recall my own bewilderment on first reading about contemplative prayer as I tried to make sense of distinctions between acquired and infused contemplation, positive and negative contemplation, active and passive contemplation—and much more. So, before we consider more carefully what contemplative prayer is and is not, it might make sense to start with the concept of contemplation.

CONTEMPLATION

To understand contemplation, think of gazing at a starry sky on a dark, cloudless night. Notice how you are looking at the stars.

Unless you are an astrophysicist or an astronomy buff, your gaze is not likely analytical. Probably it is more one of awe than analysis. Your restless sea of churning thoughts is momentarily stilled. You are filled with wonder. Rather than seeking to understand what you are seeing, you simply open yourself to something within your vision but beyond your understanding. The great Jewish rabbi Abraham Heschel describes it in this way: "The stirring in our hearts when watching the star-studded sky is something no language can declare. What smites us with unquenchable amazement is not that which we grasp and are able to convey but that which lies within our reach but beyond our grasp—the ineffable."[2]

Contemplation is a way of opening our self to the ineffable—to something that is beyond us and upon which we gaze with awe. It is seeing through eyes of wonder rather than reason. We could say that it is seeing through the eyes of a child, since contemplation is a way of knowing very familiar to children even if forgotten by most adults. Children know how to stand in awe of the small, ordinary things in their world and see the specialness that they contain. As a child you knew how to open yourself to the world and engage with it in a way that was uncluttered by thinking and talking. You knew how to allow yourself to be captured by something, not simply think about it. You knew how to let it get you rather than you simply get it.[3] And you knew how to remain wordlessly with whatever was holding your attention. This knowing by the way of wonder that comes so naturally to children is an important part of the reason that Jesus urged his followers to become like little children.

Contemplation is wordless openness to that which we consider. Gerald May describes it as "an uncluttered appreciation of existence that is free from preoccupation, preconception and interpretation."[4] This is what we experience on that starry night when, rather than seeing the sky through the lens of our thoughts and understanding, we encounter it much more directly—simply as it presents itself to us.

CONTEMPLATION AS PRAYER

We get a hint about how this becomes prayer when we notice that the English word *contemplation* is based on three components—a prefix *(con)*, a root *(templa)* and a suffix *(tion)*.[5] The root of the word—*templa*—comes from the Latin word *templum*. In Roman times the *templum* was a particular segment of the heavens, the place where God dwelled. The earthly temple was, of course, the place where one went to commune with God and experience God's presence. So, "templa" is the place where God dwells. The suffix—*tion*—means a state of being or an abiding state. We all have these. It may be a state of anxiety, cynicism or hopefulness, but Scriptures and the testimony of the saints hold out for us the possibility that it can also be a state of awareness of abiding in God. Perhaps you know occasional moments of God's loving presence. But you may wonder how you can live more constantly in that communion and blissful awareness. That brings us to the prefix—*con*—which means "with." It immediately speaks to the desire planted in our spirits to abide with God. Of course we may resist this desire to surrender and abide, but that resistance (which theologians have traditionally called sin) points to the underlying desire and would have no meaning without it. The resistance is secondary. The longing for union with God is primary.

Putting these three words together we see that contemplation is abiding with God. It is grounded in a relationship and is a form of knowing that occurs within the context of this relationship. This is how contemplation becomes contemplative prayer. It is a knowing that comes from being with and in God. Quite apart from any awareness of being in relationship to God, we can, of course, contemplate the stars, a poem or a problem. But the ground of all contemplation is our being, which is in God. Contemplation becomes prayer when we offer our open attentiveness with trust in the reality of our being in God. It becomes prayer when we open our eyes and heart not simply to the world that surrounds us but to the God who is in it and who sustains it.

Contemplative prayer is wordless, trusting openness to the God who dwells at the center of our being and at the center of the world. It is the opening of our body, mind and heart to the ultimate Mystery, who cannot be captured by either words or thoughts, but in whom we dwell and who dwells in us. It is trusting openness to the God in whom we abide, in whom we have our being. This is why I describe it as a prayer of being.

I am profoundly aware, however, how poorly these words communicate the mystery that is contained in this form of prayer. What does it mean to be with God? And what does such a prayer of being look like? Literal language is not very helpful in answering these questions. Fortunately, however, this is not the language that is used by those who know the most about contemplative prayer. When they talk about the experience of being with God in prayer, they use much more imaginative or figurative language. Seldom do they offer anything corresponding to a definition. Instead, they offer us images and metaphors—word pictures that evoke inner associations that connect us to a richness that literal language can never communicate.

Listen, therefore, to the way Christian mystics describe this prayer of being. Read each slowly, with your senses, imagination, heart and mind all open. Savor them, noticing those that touch your spirit.

Contemplative prayer is

- a blind feeling of one's own being, stretching unto God (*The Cloud of Unknowing*)
- hanging by God's thread of pure Love (Catherine of Genoa)
- continual communion through all things by quite simply doing everything in the presence of the Holy Trinity (Elizabeth of the Trinity)
- the world becoming luminous from within as one plunges breathlessly into human activity (Pierre Teilhard de Chardin)
- awakening to the presence of God, in love, in the human heart, and in the universe (Dom Bede Griffiths)
- resting in God (Gregory the Great)
- divine wakefulness with pure and naked intuition (Gregory of Nyssa)
- the mind stolen from itself by the ineffable sweetness of the Word (Bernard of Clairvaux)
- loving presence to what is (Anonymous)
- right understanding, with true longing, absolute trust, and sweet grace-giving mindfulness (Julian of Norwich)
- the mind's loving, unmixed, permanent attention to the things of God (Francis de Sales)
- seeing through exterior things, and seeing God in them (Thomas Merton)[6]

Notice how often Christian mystics mention the quality of seeing and knowing which this form of prayer involves. It is seeing what actually is, seeing that which is unknowable through the normal faculties and senses. It is a knowing that arises in love—that arises from knowing that we are in God and God is in and with us in love. It is a knowing that changes everything. Knowing God's loving presence to us, we are now able to offer loving presence to others—in fact, to everything that is. Being in stillness before this steady, secure presence then allows us to plunge breathlessly into the world with passionate engagement since being and doing are both important dimensions of being human.

BEYOND WORDS

Before we take this plunge, notice, however, the stillness that exists in this prayer of contemplative presence to God. This is the stillness of simple being—being with God in love. It reminds us of the possibility of communion in wordless presence. Being with God does not depend on words. As we have already noted, when someone is known in love, words become less and less necessary in order to maintain presence to the other. Lovers learn to just be with each other. This is exactly the way we can be with God. Intimacy demands that talk be balanced by attentive openness in silence, and only as this happens do we begin to know the deeper communion of shared presence that no longer depends on words. This is contemplative prayer in its simplest and purest form. Words are unnecessary—even distracting. From time to time words may be involved, but they are not the core of the communication. That core is openness in love. This makes communication ongoing even when words are few and far between.

The goal of contemplative prayer is not the elimination of thoughts or words. The goal is openness to God, being with God. But thoughts and words cannot bring us to God or God to us. Only faith can do that. Our part is simply what John of the Cross called passive loving receptivity—leaning toward God in faith with longing, openness and love.[7] It is by God's grace that we enter into relationship with the divine, not by means of anything we do or don't do. Our part is simply openness in faith. Contemplative prayer is not the suspension of action or the elimination of thoughts or words, but turning toward God in faith and openness. The rest is up to God.

Being with God in wordless, trusting openness cannot be reduced to a set of techniques. There are many approaches to contemplative prayer that have been practiced over the history of Christian spirituality. Each offers rich resources to the contemporary pray-er who wishes to learn to be with God in stillness. Let me describe just two of these—the Jesus Prayer and centering prayer. As we will discover, words play a part in both prayers. However, rather than providing the content of our prayer, they communicate our intent. The content of our communication remains wordless presence.

THE JESUS PRAYER

The oldest Christian contemplative prayer tradition is the one that has been the core of my personal prayer life for twenty-five years. God placed it in my path at a time when my prayers had dried up because they had stayed in my head too long. For too long they had been the result of my effort, the expression of my doing. Consequently, my spirit was arid and my longings for a deeper openness to and meeting of God intense. In the midst of that period of longing God led me to a slim little book called

The Way of a Pilgrim.[8] Written by an anonymous nineteenth-century Russian who sought out a monk of the Russian Orthodox Church, asking to be taught how to pray, it introduced me to the Jesus Prayer—"Lord Jesus Christ, Son of God, have mercy upon me, a sinner."[9] Like the pilgrim, I began to say this prayer over and over throughout the day. At first, I was very aware that I was doing something, not simply being. I was quite conscious of my effort to keep repeating the words of this prayer, bringing myself back to this task whenever I became aware that I had stopped praying the words and drifted off into something else. But as I did so, the prayer soon began to emerge from a deeper place within me and was no longer simply the result of my effort. It had begun to sink from my mind to my heart, from consciousness to my unconscious.

As I continued to learn more about this prayer through reading and work with a spiritual director, I then began to coordinate the phrases of the prayer with my breathing:

"Lord Jesus Christ, Son of God"—inhalation
"Have mercy upon me, a sinner"—exhalation

This was a powerful way of allowing the prayer to sink even deeper into my being. Now I really began to know it as a prayer of being. It was as if the prayer began to pray itself. Whenever I am free from distraction, the prayer begins to emerge synchronized with my breathing. No longer simply a mental prayer, it becomes a body prayer or, as I sometimes think of it, a breath prayer.

Then, like the pilgrim author of the book, I began to pray the Jesus Prayer as I walked. He took this much further than me. The book is his journal, recording his experience with God during his walking pilgrimage back and forth across the length and breadth of Russia. I walk much less than he, but my practice and experience have been much like his. As I walk I simply allow the prayer to fall into place with my breathing. As my breathing speeds up I notice that the prayer begins to slow down. At those points, without effort, a new rhythm of breathing and praying emerges:

"Lord Jesus Christ"—inhalation
"Son of God"—exhalation
"Have mercy upon me"—inhalation
"A sinner"—exhalation

Most of the time, however, I am unaware of praying. No longer do I even have to start praying it when I walk. As soon as I begin to walk, I simply notice the prayer emerging from within me. It is now the prayer of the Spirit. My role is simply to allow the Spirit to pray through me as I spend the time with God. No longer is it something that I do. It has become something that God does in me.

Because the prayer is not my own, I make no demands on the form it takes. Occasionally it emerges as a song. Without intention, I suddenly notice that I am singing—usually silently—the words of the prayer to a tune that I usually do not know but which the Spirit obviously has given me for that moment. Other times I find the whole prayer being reduced to one or two of its phrases. Usually this involves a repetition, still coordinated with my breathing, of "Lord, have mercy." Other times it is distilled down to a single word—"Lord." I make no effort to pray or to keep my thoughts focused on God. As soon as I become aware that I am thinking of someone or something, I simply release that thought with the next repetition of "Lord, have mercy." I lift whoever or whatever has come to my mind to God and leave the person or situation there. My prayer is a request for mercy, a request that God would bless this person or situation. I simply say "Lord, have mercy" and let go of whatever I was thinking of, returning to stillness before God. And I allow the Spirit to continue praying through me.

You do not have to be an Eastern Orthodox Christian to make this prayer yours. Nor do you have to pray it while walking, or with any effort to coordinate it with your breathing. Just let it take the form in you that is the gift of the Spirit. Doing so, you will come to know why the Jesus Prayer is so prized within the Eastern Orthodox Church. I am deeply thankful to God that this part of our Christian family has preserved this rich prayer tradition for us, making it available to those of us who long to open ourselves to God in a prayer of being.

The Jesus Prayer is appropriately described as a mantra prayer (which means a prayer based on the repetition of word or short phrase), of which there are a number of other famous Christian examples. Mantras are simply words or phrases of sacred intent that collect the mind and invoke divine presence. In Christian prayer the repeated phrase is, like the Jesus Prayer, often drawn from Scripture.[10] But this is not essential, and there are many possible short phrases that can be constructed and offered as Christian prayer, because they are offered to God in faith and openness with the intent of deepening that faith and openness. Saint Francis urged his disciples to pray "My God and my all," repeating this over and over again until it emerges as a prayer of the heart and spirit. Father John Main, the developer of a prayer tradition called Christian meditation, recommends a similar use of the word *Maranatha* (Come, Lord Jesus).

Any short phrase is suitable. I know many people who have

developed their own, based on their own spiritual tradition or personal theology. Someone recently told me that his prayer phrase was "The Lord is my Shepherd." Someone else that I know uses a self-composed phrase, "Deeply loved by God." The mantra simply helps concentration, enabling us to go beyond thoughts, even holy thoughts. Remember—the goal is to spend time in unworded stillness and openness with God, not to think about God. This is not the time to meditate on your phrase. It is the time to use it as a way of setting aside your thoughts and simply being present to the God who is present to you.

CENTERING PRAYER

Whereas the Jesus Prayer involves focusing attention through the repetition of a prayer word, the other major tradition of Christian contemplative prayer—centering prayer—is based quite simply on releasing whatever thoughts enter the mind. Thomas Keating calls it a prayer of intention, not attention.[11] It starts with an intention of being totally open to God. When this is present, all that we must then do is offer our consent to the presence and action of God within us in whatever form it arises.[12]

The origins of centering prayer are also ancient. Oral tradition traces it back to the fourth-century desert father John Cassian. Its earliest and clearest written expression is found in the fourteenth-century medieval text *The Cloud of Unknowing*.[13] By this time it had become an important prayer tradition in the monastic life of the Western church. It was, however, not until the twentieth century that it gained widespread use by laity, which largely occurred through the writing and teaching of two Cistercian monks—Basil Pennington and Thomas Keating.[14]

Centering prayer cannot be reduced to a method, but there is a framework for its practice. That framework can be summarized in two short sentences:

Be with God within.
Use a prayer word to stay and return.[15]

To expand on this slightly, let me organize the practice around four guidelines that I find helpful: (1) select a love word or a prayer word for God, (2) sit relaxed and quiet, (3) turn your attention to the Lord present within you, and (4) whenever you become aware of anything, gently return to the Lord with your prayer word.

1. Begin by selecting a word that connects you to the Lord in love or that reminds you of your intention. This might be a favorite name for God (Abba, Lord, Jesus, Father, Love, etc.), or it might simply be a word that opens you to God or reminds you of why you are doing what you are doing (*trust, still, open* or *let go*). Don't worry if it takes some time for you to settle on this word. But once you do, allow it to be your prayer word. It is not a magical talisman that should be expected to produce a desired spiritual effect. The word itself is neutral. It is your intent that makes it sacred.

2. Then, as you settle yourself in stillness, offer a brief worded prayer asking for help and declaring your intention of being present to the God who is present to you in love.

3. Now turn your heart toward God. Be open in faith and love to the One who dwells in the center of your being. You do not need to do anything to capture God's attention or love. You do not even need to think of or speak to God. Simply be with God in love.

4. When you become aware that you are thinking of some-

thing—regardless of whatever that might be—gently say your prayer word once as a way of releasing whatever was in your mind and returning to being with God in stillness. Do not keep repeating the word as a mantra. Just allow the single utterance of it to turn you away from the distraction and toward the Lord. Note that even thoughts about God count as distractions. This isn't the time to think about God. It's time to simply be open to and with God.

Most teachers of centering prayer suggest daily centering sessions of twenty minutes. I find that when beginning the practice, five to ten minutes is often sufficient. As with any form of contemplative prayer, it is important to first find a place where you can be still and uninterrupted. Although it would be hard to develop the prayer practice without some degree of silence and solitude, once the prayer has become your own, you will find that it is quite possible to center yourself in God's presence even when in the midst of the flow of a busy day. Simply draw in a deep breath, offer your prayer word and let go of all that swirls within you as you allow yourself to sink into God's loving presence.

I recall a mother of two preschool children once telling me how thankful she was to God that she had cultivated the practice of centering prayer before the birth of her children because she couldn't imagine now being able to find the space to do so. However, she said, she was able to daily snatch moments when she could still practice it in a truncated way, quickly settling herself back into Jesus' loving presence and placing all the stress and distress that she was carrying into his hands. These moments were, she said, what allowed her to keep her sanity by grounding her in the presence of God.

The theology of centering prayer is surrender and self-emptying *(kenosis)*.[16] Self-emptying is, of course, seen most clearly in Jesus. Recall the hymn quoted by Paul in his teaching on humility (Philippians 2:5-8):

> Make your own the mind of Christ Jesus:
> His state was divine,
> Who, being in the form of God,
> did not count equality with God something to be grasped
> But he emptied himself,
> taking the form of a slave,
> becoming as human beings are;
> and being in every way like a human being,
> he was humbler yet,
> even to accepting death,
> death on a cross.

Centering prayer is practice in this sort of self-emptying. It is letting go of all those things that anchor our identity in our interior dialogue, thoughts, daydreams and fantasies. It is practice in surrender. But because it is an act of surrender to a person, it is relational. It is not simply a mental technique. It is prayer, a prayer of being with God in wordless, trusting openness of self.

WHAT TO EXPECT

Nothing can ruin prayer more than inappropriate expectations. This is particularly true of contemplative prayer.

Don't confuse contemplative prayer (or any prayer) with experience. You may have a mystical experience of union with God or an ecstatic sense of divine presence, but most people who pray contemplatively for a lifetime do not. This does not mean that they did something wrong. The essence of contemplative prayer is not an experience of God but simply spending time with God. We ruin prayer if we are constantly examining what we are getting from it. Cynthia Bourgeault reminds us that "what goes on in those silent depths during the times of Centering is no one's business, not even your own; it is between your innermost being and God."[17] So, as much as you can, ignore what's going on. The only thing to seek in contemplative prayer is God.

Try not to think of silence as an empty container into which God pours content. Instead, accept silence as its own form of communication. Thomas Keating reminds us of something long taught by Christian mystics when he asserts that "silence is God's first language; everything else is a poor translation."[18] In order to learn that language, we must learn to be still and to rest in God. Contemplative prayer is God's language school— the place where we learn God's language of silence and learn true spiritual rest.

What should you expect to achieve from contemplative prayer? If you are attempting to use it for relaxation or mental calming, you should expect failure and frustration. As soon as thoughts are released, new ones rush in to fill the vacuum produced by silence. While this does offer you the gift of endless opportunities to practice surrender, it will become quite exasperating if you are using contemplative prayer as a way to attain inner serenity. But as you continue to release these thoughts, you should expect to receive the gift of growth in the virtues and the fruit of the Spirit, as well as a transformational encounter with both God and yourself. The goal is God, not growth. But any genuine encounter with God involves an encounter with self, and when this occurs within the regular practice of contemplative prayer, it will change you in deep ways.

The invitation to contemplative prayer is an invitation to

walk the path of pure faith—a path that demands we persevere in making our self available to God in stillness and silence without regard for what we are getting out of it. Thomas Keating likes to say that we don't have to feel it, but we do have to practice it. That practice is simple, but it is extremely demanding. The demands, however, are not what you might expect. What it requires is not so much resolve as faith. Yes, we must choose to make space for God. But the real challenge is following the path of dark faith that contemplative prayer demands— dark because we must walk without seeing. What we encounter in contemplative prayer cannot be seen by the natural faculties. It can only be seen by faith. Contemplative prayer—like all prayer—demands faith. Without faith it wouldn't be prayer!

CULTIVATING PRAYERFUL BEING

Contemplative prayer should not be undertaken as a spiritual self-improvement project. Nor should it be explored simply out of curiosity. Allow longings to guide you into this practice and then trust that the Spirit, who is the source of those deep longings, will guide the process.

If you long for deeper intimacy with God—not simply more intense spiritual highs but genuine knowing of God that comes from being with God in stillness— consider this an invitation to contemplative prayer that has been placed in your spirit by the Spirit of God. Your job now is simply to make space for God in stillness. Perhaps you have been making intentional space for

God already, but filling that with words and activities. Contemplative space is more open than this normal sort of instrumental space in which we are trying to accomplish something, even something spiritual. My wife likes to describe contemplative prayer as wasting time with God. Don't expect results. Simply give regular blocks of time—daily if possible or regularly if not—to God in stillness and unworded presence to the God who is present to you.

Let me offer three suggestions about how to use this time.

1. Start with *lectio divina* (as discussed in chap. 3). Remember the basic rhythm of this dance with the Spirit—silence and the Word. Take that small portion of Scripture and listen for God's word to you for this day. This is an excellent way of moving into contemplative prayer. Attend, ponder, respond and then simply be with God in rest and love.

2. Once your practice of *lectio* is established, consider adding the Jesus Prayer. For the first few months, offer this prayer in physical stillness, not while walking. Make no effort to coordinate it with your breathing. Simply repeat the prayer in an unhurried manner for as much time as you set aside. Start with ten minutes each day—perhaps at the end of your *lectio divina*. Or, if you are having tea or coffee by yourself sometime during the day, make this a time for the Jesus Prayer. Be gentle

with yourself when you notice that your mind has strayed and that you again have been thinking about something or other. Rather than wasting time and energy by slapping yourself on the wrist, simply speak your prayer word and return to the prayer. Be prepared for the fact that it will feel like practice for a while—often for at least a month of daily use. But with practice, it will recede into the background and become a durable framework for your encounters with God in unworded stillness.

3. If, after a few weeks, the Jesus Prayer is becoming a rich place of stillness before God, continue its use and do not be distracted by considering adding centering prayer. If however, it does not feel like it has helped you be with God, set it aside for the moment and try centering prayer. Some people find one of these a deeply natural way of being with God, but not the other. Never try to develop them at the same time, and be careful of being overly willful in taking either up as a project. Trying to make contemplative prayer work for you just because it sounds interesting or because you know someone who is finding it a blessing will always lead to frustration. After an introduction to either, simply wait for the Spirit to invite you to explore one or the other as a framework for being with God. But also be open to the possibility that the way you can be open to God in stillness and presence may take its own unique form.

Like any prayer, there is no one correct form that contemplative prayer should take. I know people who simply sit in stillness with a candle burning or with music playing, and this is the external face of their inner presence to God. Others find this time of being with God happens best as they clean the house, do yard work or take care of other routine chores. Brother Lawrence cultivated stillness and rest in the presence of God while he was washing dishes.[19] I know many people—women and men—who find knitting or embroidery to be an extremely rich context for contemplative prayer. I have met others who have told me that they find themselves most comfortably resting in God's presence when doing a crossword or puttering in a garage or basement workshop. Contemplative prayer does not require isolation or inactivity. All it requires is being with God in unworded inner stillness.

The important thing in contemplative prayer is to not reduce it to a technique or method. There are things that you can do to support a posture of restful stillness with God, but don't allow yourself to be distracted by those things. At its core it is much more a matter of letting go than doing something. Perhaps you will find elements of the Jesus Prayer or centering prayer helpful, but discover your own unique adaptation that comes to you as a gift of the Spirit. Thank God for this and do not worry about being a purist. Remember, the point is being with the Master, not mastering a practice.

LIFE AS PRAYER, PRAYER AS LIFE

BY NOW IT SHOULD BE OBVIOUS that prayer is so much more than praying. What we usually think of as praying—that is, offering worded prayer—is, of course, an important part of prayer. In fact, it is an essential part of it. Prayer of attention, pondering or being that lacked any communication would quickly lose its meaning as prayer. Worded prayer reminds us that prayer is personal and relational. This is what sets it apart from meditative techniques that are designed to help us achieve enlightenment or other psychological or spiritual results. But if we fail to move beyond words, prayer—and our relationship with God—will eventually grow tiresome and stagnant.

For decades I faithfully set aside time most days to read my Bible and pray. I thank God for this practice and for parents and a church that encouraged it. But eventually—I would even say inevitably—this led to a point where it was nothing more than a rather meaningless discipline. Instead of arising out of a heart that longed to be with God, it arose from a will that was stubbornly and pridefully bent on doing what I had been taught I was supposed to do. I thank God that eventually this grew boring and tedious. If it had not, I might not have noticed the longing for a deeper knowing of God that it was masking. Part of that longing was a desire to experience deeper integration within my being—for the spiritual and not-so-obviously spiritual parts to be better connected and for the spiritual parts to be moved out of the compartment in which they had been far too well contained. I longed to have a relationship with God that would be a part of my experience throughout the day regardless of what I was doing—regardless of whether or not I happened to be thinking of God, praying, or doing something religious or spiritual.

PRAYER AS RELATIONSHIP

Prayer that is reduced to technique or discipline seriously misses the fact that first and foremost, prayer expresses a relationship between us and God. And remember what Jesus said about the nature of this relationship. He said that we were his friends, not his servants (John 15:15). We are, in fact, his intimates, his inner circle of friends, those from whom he withholds nothing good, passing on to us everything that he receives from his Father. It is to this friend's presence in our life and our world that we attune our self when we offer prayers of attending. It is with this friend that we offer prayers of pondering, responding and being.

Friendship is not something we do. It is something that we might celebrate, feel gratitude for, honor and make space for, but it can never be reduced to obligations or behavior. Nor should prayer be diminished in these ways. Prayer is communion with our Beloved. It is being in love—living our lives grounded in our being in God. And it is this that makes it possible for all of life to be a prayer.

All of life is, in fact, lived in relationship to God. It is no more possible for a human to live apart from a relationship to God than it is possible for us to be our own origin. But what makes life a prayer is the cultivation of the knowing—conscious and unconscious—of being in that relationship. This knowing starts with conscious knowing. Conscious knowing of God's presence in love is the ground of ceaseless prayer. Slowly this knowing seeps into the unconscious so we no longer need to be conscious of God's presence to know in some deep place that we are in communion with our Beloved all the time, regardless of the circumstances. Contemplative prayer is the major way in which this seeping into the unconscious occurs. Being with God only in worded ways keeps us in our heads and keeps the volume of mental noise high enough that it interrupts the development of deeper knowing. Being with God in unworded stillness allows this deep knowing to develop and allows our prayers of attention, pondering and responding to flow from these deep places.

FINDING GOD IN ALL THINGS

The possibility of humans experiencing the transcendent, wholly Other is grounded in the fact that this same God is also immanent—forever connected to the material world and our experiences within it. Every experience we have involves this world in which God resides. Furthermore, since Christ is in us, not simply in the world, every experience is even more closely connected to God. In fact, it is not possible for a human to have an experience of any sort that God is not a part of. Rather than searching for God in religious or spiritual experiences, we need to remember that God is present in all of life. Every human experience has the possibility of being an encounter with God.

If you have not been accustomed to seeking God in all things and all experiences, I suspect that this notion that God is present in all of life may seem a little absurd. You may, for example, think of personal experiences of injustice or suffering that make it seem preposterous to try to find God in such places. But when God seems absent, it is we who are failing to see, and usually this is because we think that God only dwells in places of light and forget that God is also in the darkness. The Dutch Jew Etty Hillesum found God in the midst of the horrors of the Nazi roundup of Jews.[1] And even though Jesus felt like God had abandoned him in the hours of struggle in Gethsemane, he knew that his Father was, in fact, present as he opened himself to God in prayer.

Despite the testimony of the mystics who speak of the possibility of occasional direct mystical encounters with God that seem unmediated by other experiences, normally we meet God in mediated ways—in Scripture, in the Eucharist, in other people, in the midst of life experiences. Exactly where God is in most experiences may be far from obvious, but this should not blind us to the truth that God is, in fact, present. It should, rather, encourage us to seek the sort of spiritual discernment that allows us to see what truly is.

Discernment is important because of the multidimensionality of human experience. Learning to find God in all things comes with practice in spiritual attentiveness, but it also comes through discernment. This brings us back to the crucial role of the examen—something that perhaps you began to practice after reading chapter four. Any experience can be examined to discover the presence of God. Learning to become aware of God's presence in the midst of our daily experience is to know that we are not alone. It is to know that God is indeed with us. What could be more blessed than that!

Being attentive to where God is in the circumstances of our lives is a rich way of allowing our knowing of God's loving presence to move into those deep places in the soul that make all of life a prayer. Simply asking, "Where might God be in this circumstance or experience?" as a pondering prayer opens us to attentiveness to the Spirit that will reveal the presence of our Beloved.

Just this morning I received an email from a friend telling me that his wife had experienced a heart attack and come through open-heart surgery. He spoke of the cascading fears he had been experiencing and of his anxieties about their future. But he also spoke of his desire to see where God was in these events. He dared to trust that God was present in his life, and this meant that God was somewhere in the midst of these unwelcome circumstances, accompanying him and his wife and leading them to new things.

Asking where God might be in unwelcome circumstances is quite different from asking why they happened. That question is ultimately unanswerable. But "Where were you, God, when this happened?" and "Where are you now in my experience?" are questions that can be answered—not by me but by the Spirit. The Spirit of God is the One who reveals God to us. Paul teaches that the Spirit has come to teach us to understand the gifts that God has given us (1 Corinthians 2:12). Unwelcome circumstances—such as heart attacks and other forms of suffering—are not gifts. But they may contain a gift. Don't simply ask, therefore, what you are supposed to learn from the circumstances. Rather, pray that the Spirit would help you discern the gifts of God that the circumstances contain. The core of that gift is God's presence. All knowing of God's gifts starts with knowing the Giver of all good gifts, and God's loving presence is the foundation of this knowing. So, when we ask, "Where might you be in this situation?" in prayerful attentiveness and pondering, we can be assured that God will reveal the answer.[2]

THE WELCOMING PRAYER

This trust is also the basis of the welcoming prayer, a prayer practice that has developed in recent years as a spin-off of centering prayer and is also an excellent way to move toward all of life being a prayer. Welcoming prayer provides a framework for how to respond to the emotional upset that accompanies unwelcome experiences with a spirit of surrender. It is, therefore, a very practical way of responding prayerfully to the things that inevitably happen in life that we would not naturally choose. It involves a three-step process: focus, welcome and letting go.[3]

Before we can welcome an emotion, we must bring it into consciousness. We must face it directly and feel it as a sensation in our bodies. If, for example, you are anxious, the first step is simply to be present to that anxiety. Notice where your body holds this anxiety. Perhaps your stomach is in a knot. Or possibly your face is flushed, your breathing accelerated or your mouth dry. Keep your focus on the place you first notice, wherever it is. Do not judge, analyze or try to control whatever you are experiencing. In fact, do not even try to change it. Just be aware of the sensations in your body. This is the key to the entire process of surrender, because we can only release things we have first acknowledged.

The next step—welcome—seems strange when the emotion

is instinctively unwelcome. Our normal response to unpleasant emotions is to do whatever we can to push them out of our awareness. Something quite remarkable happens when, instead of following this well-worn path, we welcome them as a guest in the home of our self. When resistance is replaced by welcome, we remove the power of these unchosen events to disturb our peace. Once we respond to them with hospitality, their disruptiveness begins to diminish—sometimes with astounding speed. The simple act of gently saying, "Welcome, anxiety" (or whatever disruptive emotion has suddenly arrived on the scene) expresses a soul hospitality that grounds us in the present and in our body, and refuses to allow the external experience to chase us out of presence.

It is important to recognize, however, that what we are welcoming is our inner response to the present moment, not the whole set of circumstances that might surround it. For example if you have just been told that you have a brain tumor, it is not the tumor that you welcome but the fear or anger that might accompany this news. The surrender that is being encouraged through this practice of welcoming prayer is an inner release of that which disturbs your peace and compromises your openness in trust to God.

Letting go—the core of surrender—is the final step in this process of welcoming prayer. What we must release is not simply the negative feelings but also the assumption that to be happy we need to be in control. This is a lie. Our attempt to be in control of our lives—captains of our own ship and masters of our own destiny—inevitably leads to our unhappiness. It is futile because we are not God. What we need to release, therefore, is our inordinate attachment to our desire for control.

Life brings us a steady flow of opportunities to practice

choosing surrender. But what makes this act of surrender prayer is its interpersonal context. Surrender is not simply a mental technique designed to make us happy. If it is surrender to God, it is prayer. What makes this possible is faith in God. Surrender is entrusting to God things over which we have no control. Every time we do so we exercise faith in action. Every time we do so we are in prayer.

LIVING WITH OPENNESS TO GOD

Prayer is living with openness to God. Our life becomes a prayer, and our prayer becomes our life as we begin to live with this openness as the core posture of our hearts.

The person from whom I have learned the most about living with openness to God is Basil Pennington. First through his books and then through the blessing of a close friendship, I was able to witness a life that was truly open to God. His was a life of prayer. Of course, being a monk has certain advantages in making all of life a prayer. He was always quick to acknowledge this, and was deeply appreciative of the way the rhythms of the life of his Cistercian community supported prayer.[4] But I came to see that his times of prayer were far from limited to these many hours each day spent in *lectio divina,* the Liturgy of the Hours or centering prayer. These things simply served as the framework that allowed his prayerful, attentive openness to God to flow out into the rest of the day.

He described openness to God as having both an input and an output dimension. By "input" he meant making space for God in stillness to attend to God's Word and allow it to seep into our heart. This he did through daily *lectio divina*—prayerful attentiveness to small portions of the Word and then soaking in this by means of prayerful pondering. By "output" he meant the responding and being movements of prayer. "The first thing to do in responding to God's presence and Word," he repeatedly told me, "is to notice what God is doing and to keep out of God's way. The second is to align ourselves with and participate in God's transformational actions in the world." God is active and present in the world. Our job is not to bring God to the world. That has already happened. That is the good news of creation and the incarnation. Our job is to follow the Spirit into the world and be part of what God is doing there to establish God's kingdom of justice and love.

This practice of attending to where God is and what God is doing has changed my life. I no longer have any confidence that I know what an individual who comes to me for spiritual or psychological help needs, and exactly what the priorities of their life should be—at least not without first considering where God is already in the person's life and what God is doing to nudge him or her toward fuller and deeper life. I really am convinced that I do not need to bring God to anyone. But after being sure that I don't get in the road of what God is doing, I do have an important role, and that is to come alongside the person and make myself available to support God's work in and through him or her in the world.

Living with openness to God is transformational. It changes us, and God flowing through us changes the world. The core dynamic of this life of transformational prayer is receiving God's love and then passing it on to the world. It is as simple as breathing in and then breathing out—we take in love and then we pass it on. This is a life of openness to God.

Each time I was with Basil Pennington, and at the end of every single email exchange, he would say to me, "Let us continue to hold each other in prayer." After hearing this from him a number of times, and fearing that I might not be living up to its implicit promise, I asked what this meant to him. His answer was disarmingly uncomplicated: "Everyone I hold in my heart in love, I lift up to God in prayer every time that I turn to God with openness of heart."

Our job is to allow our self to be loved and then to hold others in love that passes on to them what we have received from God. This is a life of prayer.

HOLISTIC PRAYER AND OPENNESS TO GOD

Holistic prayer is prayer that includes our entire beings. Each of the four major prayer paths we have discussed features one of these dimensions. But each also moves us toward others. For example, allowing our mind and spirit to turn toward God as we hear church bells or see a lighted candle begins as a prayer of attention but then invites a prayer of response. The response may be to pause and turn our attention toward God or to allow our spirit to draw sustenance from a moment of simply being aware of God's presence. Allowing our hunger during a fast to draw our attention toward God reflects the same twofold dynamic. On the other hand, meditatively walking the Stations of the Cross—something that has long been a popular Catholic (both Roman and Anglican) form of prayer but which is currently being discovered by many Protestants—is a prayer that begins with walking (response) but is primarily an act of meditation (pondering). Here the response supports the pondering. Sitting in silence while we allow our heart to be drawn toward God by the periodic gentle repetition of a love name for God works in much the same way. The response of speaking God's name is in support of a contemplative prayer of being in stillness before God.

This is the way prayer works as we bring more and more of our self to the divine encounter. We may start with just our mind, but if we are willing, our heart will also be naturally drawn in and vice versa. Or we may begin with attention, but awareness strongly pulls for a response. The flow among the various dimensions of our being is as natural as the way in which they work together to form us as whole beings. It is only when we have artificial and limited ideas about what prayer is and isn't that it takes on truncated expressions.

But if prayer is to be grounded in reality it is essential that we start where we are, not where we think we should be. Perhaps it feels like too big a step to make all of life a prayer. If so, start where you are. Talk with God about that in a pondering prayer. Be honest in your assessment, but don't give in to a temptation to guilt or self-recrimination. Those postures are not prayer, because they involve shifting your attention from God to yourself. A more prayerful posture is simply to speak to God about where you are in your prayer life.

Let me again try to make this practical. Consider the following suggestions if you wish to cultivate a life more characterized by openness to God in all dimensions of your being.

1. Reviewing what you have read in this book, notice the nudges that the Spirit of God may have given you. Some approaches to prayer may seem too far from your comfort zone or present life to be helpful. But others may have caught your attention. Trust that the Spirit of God was guiding your attention and stirring your spirit in response to what you have read. Take seriously, therefore, the things that caught your attention. Talk with God about how you might respond. And be sure to respond.

2. Consider also which of the four faces of holistic prayer are most lacking for you. The goal is not balance but wholeness. Openness to God means opening all of the channels of your self. Holistic prayer is bringing your whole self to the divine encounter. Take note of which parts have the most minimal presence in your times of presence to God. Be intentional about bringing more of your self into the circle of love that is prayer communion with God. Doing so will open you more fully to the grace of God and allow that grace to flow through you more completely.

3. Also consider whether any of the practices discussed in this chapter represent invitations of the Spirit to

move prayer beyond formal times of prayer to the rest of your life. Follow your longings on this. If nothing in you feels drawn to making all of your life a prayer, wait—without feeling guilty—for the Spirit to lead you in this direction. If, however, your heart longs for a deeper, ongoing communion with your Beloved, allow the Spirit to guide you toward a life that is prayer. Consider how you could live with more loving openness to God, allowing God's love to flow through you to the world. Perhaps the welcoming prayer would be a way for you to remain more open to God and be less easily distracted by emotional reactions. The ideas discussed in this chapter are only a start on the journey of life as prayer. Prayer is so much more than anything I have been able to say about it. It is the heartbeat of the Christian life. Nothing less will ultimately satisfy the deepest desires of your heart.

9

TRANSFORMATIONAL PRAYER

TALK OF TRANSFORMATION RUNS the risk of being dismissed as hyperbole. In terms of personal change, most of us know only the frustrations and extremely modest progress we have experienced in our spiritual and psychological self-improvement projects. Perhaps all you have ever known are small incremental steps forward, followed by at least as many often bigger steps backward. Maybe over a longer period of your life you can see growth, but you feel suspicious about calling it transformation. Even when you think of family members, friends or acquaintances, it may still be hard to think of anyone you would describe as having undergone change of a magnitude to warrant such grand language.

If this is true in general, how much more unrealistic it must sound to speak of transformational prayer. It might seem like a pious thing to say, but likely it is not very believable. If you are able to identify meaningful changes that have occurred in your inner world, and particularly if these came from hard work done in counseling or psychotherapy, it might be difficult for you to imagine that anything comparable could ever result from prayer. But can it really? And if it can, what exactly is transformed and how does it happen?

I am convinced that truly opening our self to God has enormous potential for the transformation of our inner life, changes that can then ripple out through our body into our behavior and the world. But it is inner change that most interests me as a psychologist and as a spiritual guide, because I know that when change starts in the inner self it inevitably flows out to the rest of life in one way or another. Because all true prayer involves opening our self to God, all prayer is capable of being the means of grace by which God does this work in us. But the prayer that gives God the most penetrating access to our depths is offered in stillness. Prayer that includes a contemplative dimension has potential to reorganize our interior landscape in ways that we can not imagine—and all for the good!

THE CONTEMPLATIVE DIMENSION OF PRAYER

I speak of a contemplative dimension to prayer to underscore the fact that contemplative prayer is not so much a type of prayer as something that should be a component of all prayer. It is the silence and space for stillness before God that supports genuine presence and openness to God. A life of prayer that is exclusively built around attending, pondering or responding will not have the same transformational possibilities as that which also includes times for simply being with God. Sadly, it is this contemplative dimension that is most lacking from prayer. Communal prayer seldom leaves sufficient space for stillness before God in silence. Even liturgical prayer often leaves inadequate space for silence, and nonliturgical worship experiences are, of course, usually infamously devoid of silence. Intentional times of personal prayer are often rushed and reduced to the basics of petitions, intercession and possibly an expression or two of gratitude. All this is certainly worthy of being called prayer. But lacking the contemplative dimension, it is not holistic prayer and it will not be transformational.

Speaking of prayer that includes this contemplative dimension, Thomas Keating describes it as "a process of interior transformation, a conversation initiated by God and leading, if we consent, to divine union."[1] The way we see ourselves, others, the world and God will change in this process. Our ability to perceive and relate to the divine presence will also change dramatically. It will transform our heart and mind as an awareness of our being in relationship with God slowly comes to replace the ordinary background noise of thoughts.

According to the fourth-century desert father Evagrius Ponticus, "Prayer is the laying aside of thoughts."[2] This reminds us that contemplation in prayer is not so much the absence of thoughts as detachment from them. This is what we offer to God when we are open—not just in our mind but also in our heart, body, emotions, spirit and whole being. And chief among the thoughts that we release as we seek to simply be with God in stillness and inner silence are evaluative wonderings about our prayer experience. Nothing fills us with more self-preoccupation than appraising the shape our prayer is taking. As Anthony of the Desert reminds us, "Perfect prayer is not to know that you are praying."[3] It is to be mindlessly present to God—not present in an anti-intellectual or nonreflective way, but present in a way that is not limited by the constraints of self-consciousness. This is a presence to God that opens us in remarkably deep ways when it is offered with our consent to God's gracious work in us.

TRANSFORMATIONAL PRESENCE

Most people are surprised when they offer whatever stillness they have to God in a prayer of openness and discover that the resulting encounter is not simply an encounter with God. It is also an encounter with their self. Of course, this is what makes the encounter potentially transformational. It would not even be an encounter if you were not present. Nonetheless, it can be quite disconcerting if you are attempting to lay aside your thoughts and create space for God, and discover that this space keeps being filled with all the inner things you have been avoiding. You might, for example, go on a silent retreat and be frustrated by how little inner silence you experience. Instead of quiet and calm your inner world is full of sound and fury—old anxieties and conflicts that have been lingering at the edges of consciousness now coming to the front burner and uninvited memories and feelings bubbling to the surface. This is the price of admission to presence to God. That price is presence to self.

Deep prayer that contains a contemplative dimension will always require hospitality to your deep self—that is, to the deep parts of your self. Pray for the grace to receive whatever might arise in you, and then gently release it into God's hands. That which arises might come with a flood of emotional intensity. Sometimes being still before self and God releases a torrent of emotions. Tears may be intermixed with joy and sadness as repressed memories and fragments of past experience burst into consciousness. This unloading of the unconscious can be frightening, but it is a sign that God is at work in your depths.[4] This isn't the time to try to understand the things that float to the surface. Instead it is the time to simply release them to God. But as you note their presence, you become aware of what exists within you, and you have an opportunity to get a peek at the deep hidden work of healing that God is doing in your soul. This is a work of divine therapy.

It is very important to remember that the goal is not stillness. Any stillness that develops is the gift of God. Nor is this a process of self-therapy. Any healing that occurs is a byproduct, not the goal. Remember, this is prayer. The goal is simply to be totally open to God and to consent to God's presence and action within you.

DIVINE THERAPY

I have had many opportunities to witness the transformational possibilities of prayer. Let me briefly describe just one. A monk, who I will call Father John, contacted me after reading several of my books and asked if I would accompany him on a journey of healing.[5] Having spent nearly fifty years in the contemplative context of monastic life, he was far from a novice in stillness before himself and God. He knew how to open himself in contemplative prayer and knew how transformational it could be. However, encountering some new and quite deep wounds in the context of a friendship, he knew that he needed fresh and even deeper inner healing.

His first request to me was to help him discern whether he should go to a psychotherapist as a way to deal with these concerns or whether it was appropriate to turn to the healing process he knew best—contemplative prayer. What he wanted from me, he said, was help in keeping honest. He gave me a candid report of his relationship with his friend and described the old fault lines in his personal story that had been reactivated by the experience. He said that he wanted to be sure that he did not avoid facing things he knew he needed to face and that if psychotherapy was the best way to do this he was very willing to proceed in this direction. I was impressed with his openness and honesty. And so I told him that I saw no reason not to accept the inner invitation he was sensing from the Spirit to open himself in stillness before God. I also accepted his invitation to journey with him, looking over his shoulder, as it were, to help him ensure that the healing was deep enough to help him move ahead in his life and ministry.

And so for the next several years we met regularly, and Father John told me of his experience in prayer. He spoke of what came to mind when he was present in stillness to himself and God, and he described his repeated acts of simple release of these things to God. He did his best to keep his focus on God, not himself or his needs and desires for healing. But whatever he became aware of, he named and released into God's hands. I was not the director of the process, simply a witness. And what I witnessed was the way the Spirit led him through the many layers of himself, and of his personal history that needed to be part of the healing process.

The journey was not organized in the sort of systematic manner in which one might undertake self-exploration. It took him back to childhood experiences and relationships, invited him to revisit his sense of calling associated with his original entrance to the monastery, and brought him back in contact with relational conflicts and wounds that had occurred over the course of his life. The movement through these and many other dimensions of his life was far from linear. It was also far from easy. Father John found himself revisiting issues he had assumed were resolved as the Spirit walked him through the corridors of his life. But as he did, we both saw evidence of increasing inner freedom. I sensed openness to grace and a willingness to allow it to flow through him in a way that seemed to have been blocked when I first met him. Others closest to him in his community, including his abbot, affirmed that he had come into a season of deeper peace, joy and vitality. It was indeed a work of inner transformation through prayer—certainly not the result of clever interventions on my part and not simply even the result of praying for healing. It was the result of spending time in stillness before and with God, and allowing God's healing grace to penetrate and saturate his depths.

To be open to God is to be open to the Infinite, and this means to be open to infinite possibilities. Remember, prayer is not designed to change God. Its purpose is to change us. Openness to the Infinite means infinite possibilities of transformation.

FREEING LOGJAMS IN OUR OPENNESS TO GOD
Perhaps the best way to understand the transformational possibilities of contemplative prayer is to describe them in terms of the removal of blocks to openness to God. Each of us has our own logjams—things that obstruct the channels of our self that need to be opened if we are to experience the fullness of the life of God. They are our signature sins—the unique things that too often lead us to turn away from rather than toward God. But calling them sins can be misleading because these are not so much behaviors as states of being. They are deeply embedded in our psychology, theology and spiritual practices.

There are many psychological logs that can block our openness to God. Anything that keeps us self-preoccupied functions in this way, and most psychopathology does exactly this. Our addictions, our anxieties, our unresolved conflicts, our unhealed traumatic experiences and other wounds, our fears and much more tend to close us in upon ourselves and impair deep and genuine opening of our self not just to others but to the ultimate Other. How could we, for example, ever hope for the trust to abandon ourselves to God if we do not have the experience of another human who is trustworthy? And how could we hope to be attentive to God if our unfinished inner business is so preoccupying as to make us incapable of being genuinely attentive to others or the world. Often it will be through psychotherapy that God's grace can best flow into our life to heal these wounds and flush out the logjams. Wounds that are received in an interpersonal context usually require a human corrective interpersonal context for their healing, and a trained counselor or psychotherapist is often uniquely equipped to offer the necessary accompaniment and guidance on this journey. But don't fail to take advantage of the healing possibilities of divine therapy through prayer—either when combined with psychotherapy or spiritual direction, or, on some occasions, on its own.

Our psychological logjams are often closely connected with theological ones because we tend to forge our personal theology in the hearth of our wounded self. To understand this it is important to recognize the difference between our formal theology and our functional theology. To illustrate this let me briefly describe someone I know—a seminary graduate who has spent his adult life studying and reading good theology, but whose actual views of God were dramatically different from his formal beliefs. Tom, as I will call him, contacted me after reading one of my books and asked if I could work with him to help him move toward more inner freedom and outer authenticity. He felt attracted by the vision of being his own true self, but sabotaged by things that kept him stuck and in bondage to his personal history.

Hearing about his longstanding conflict with a distant and

emotionally nonsupportive father, I asked him about his views of God. What he told me could have come straight out of a textbook of theology. He spoke of God as love, wisdom, majesty, power, grace and several other wonderfully lofty ideals. I knew I needed to reframe the question, and so I then asked, "But what is your experience of God—how you actually see and feel about and relate to God?" "That," he said, "is quite different."

Tom then went on to tell me that although he was loath to admit it, he couldn't shake himself from the sense that God was capricious, untrustworthy, controlling, distant and never satisfied with whatever we offer. This was his functional theology. It was his actual, working view of God. Obviously it needed to be changed if he were to be, as he longed to be, more open to God. And such change came as he began to deal with the psychological issues that had been spilling over onto God, and as he learned to trust—for the first time in his life—being with God in nondefensive openness and trust. Over time this flushed out both the psychological and theological logjams that were the cause of his stuckness and lack of openness to God.

Rigidly hanging onto spiritual practices that no longer bring us life can also block our openness to God. I have already shared some of the ways this has been part of my own story, but this is a dynamic that I have seen in many others as well. I am struck by how often people who describe prayer practices that no longer bring them into contact with God are unwilling to let them go and find fresh ways of opening themselves to God in prayer. Often they have been taught about the importance of persisting in prayer or not being concerned about what they seem to get out of prayer. There is value in this teaching. But it is also important to recognize the seasons of the spiritual life and to allow forms of practice that no longer bring life to die so others may take root and sprout up as fresh green expressions of life.

Prayer is an invitation to come to God in openness and trust, and God provides everything that we need to do this. Sometimes this provision of what we need comes in the form of other people (spiritual friends and professional helpers) and sometimes it comes more directly from God. But always the invitation from God to us is the same—to turn to God with whatever measure of openness and trust we have, and allow God's life to flow into ours. As we do so, divine love reveals the obstacles in our depths that block our openness to God, and if we are willing to release these obstacles, slowly they are transformed into means of grace. As grace begins to seep into those places of former brokenness, we begin to experience the fullness of life that exists in God.

PRAYING AND LIVING THESE TRUTHS

Take a moment to ponder these transformational possibilities. Notice again your longing for God. Don't lose sight of this. It is the leash by which God draws you toward the openness and transformation that you seek. Notice what things stir in you as you ponder your deepest spiritual desires and the posture of openness in prayer I have been describing throughout the book. Talk with a trusted spiritual friend about how you feel led to respond. And then allow yourself to respond in whatever ways are suggested by the Spirit.

The transformational possibilities of prayer are based in allowing God's grace and love to flow into us and then through us into a needy, hurting world. It is watching as our being is transformed into the likeness of Christ and all our doing begins to flow out of this. It is our way of participating in God's making all things new in Christ. May both you and I know the fullness of life that comes from the openness and abandonment that saying yes to God's grand invitation to participate in this adventure involves.

NOTES

Acknowledgments
[1]Juliet Benner, *Contemplative Vision: A Guide to Christian Art and Prayer* (Downers Grove, Ill.: InterVarsity Press, 2011).

Chapter 1: More Than You Can Imagine
[1]Rosalind Rinker, *Prayer: Conversing with God* (Grand Rapids: Zondervan, 1959).

[2]I draw this understanding of prayer from the work of Bernard Lonergan, the Canadian Jesuit priest, philosopher and theologian whose philosophical and theological method centers on love. A highly accessible presentation of the implications of Lonergan's work for prayer can be found in William Johnston, *Being in Love: A Practical Guide to Christian Prayer* (New York: Harper & Row, 1989).

[3]Teresa of Ávila, *Interior Castle* (New York: Paulist, 1979).

[4]Thomas Green, *Drinking from the Dry Well* (Notre Dame, Ind.: Ave Marie Press, 1991), pp. 17-25.

Chapter 2: Preparing for the Divine Encounter
[1]Michael Casey, *Toward God: The Ancient Wisdom of Western Prayer* (Liguori, Mo.: Triumph, 1996), p. 35.

[2]Thomas Merton, *New Seeds of Contemplation* (New York: New Directions, 1961).

[3]Vladimir Lossky, *The Mystical Theology of the Eastern Church* (London: James, Clark, 1957), p. 206.

[4]Ann and Barry Ulanov, "Prayer and Personality: Prayer as Primary Speech," in *The Study of Spirituality*, ed. Cheslyn Jones, Geoffrey Wainwright and Edward Yarnold (New York: Oxford University Press, 1986), p. 28.

[5]Louis Evely, *This Man Is You* (New York: Paulist, 1964), pp. 15-16.

[6]This foundational role of knowing God's love in Christian spirituality is the reason that the first book in my trilogy on the Christian spiritual journey (*Surrender to Love* [Downers Grove, Ill.: InterVarsity Press, 2004]) focuses on personal knowing of this love.

[7]Thomas Green, *When the Well Runs Dry* (Notre Dame, Ind.: Ave Marie Press, 1979), p. 90.

[8]John of the Cross, *Dark Night of the Soul* (New York: Image, 1959).

[9]*The Cloud of Unknowing*, trans. James Walsh (New York: HarperCollins, 1981), p. 116.

Chapter 3: *Lectio Divina* and Four Classic Prayer Paths
[1]M. Basil Pennington, *A Place Apart: Monastic Prayer and Practice for Everyone* (Gar-

den City, N.Y.: Doubleday, 1983), p. 82.

[2]Pennington, *A Place Apart.* For a much fuller discussion of *lectio divina* see his more recent book *Lectio Divina: Renewing the Ancient Practice of Praying the Scriptures* (New York: Crossroad, 1998).

[3]I use the term *creation* without making any scientific assumptions, simply to refer to generative activity of the One whom the Nicene Creed refers to as "God the Father Almighty, Maker of heaven and earth." In chapter four I will have more to say about creation, and my nonscientific use of the word applies there as well.

[4]Cynthia Bourgeault, *Centering Prayer and Inner Awakening* (Cambridge, Mass.: Cowley, 2004), p. 73.

[5]Print versions of daily lectionary readings are widely available in Christian bookstores. An electronic version of The Revised Common Lectionary can be found at <http://lectionary.library.vanderbilt.edu>. Anglicans Online also has some wonderful resources, including lectionaries and various electronic versions of the daily office (http://anglicansonline.org/resources/liturgical.html). The Daily Office of the Catholic Church (organized according to both Anglican and Roman Catholic use) is also an excellent online resource (www.bookofhours.org).

[6]Margaret Silf, "Discovering Lectio Divina: Out of the Chocolate Box," *Crosspoint,* spring 2003, p. 28.

Chapter 4: Prayer as Attending

[1]Rowan Williams, *Tokens of Trust* (London: Canterbury Press Norwich, 2006), p. 35.

[2]Hafiz, *I Heard God Laughing,* trans. Daniel Ladinsky (Walnut Creek, Calif.: Sufism Reoriented, 1996), p. 91.

[3]Maltbie Babcock, "This Is My Father's World" (1901).

[4]Simone Weil, *Gravity and Grace,* trans. Emma Craufurd (New York: Routledge & Kegan Paul, 1987), p. 106.

[5]Simone Weil, *Simone Weil: An Anthology,* ed. and trans. Siân Miles (New York: Grove, 1986), p. 212.

[6]I will have more to say about the important role of thinking in prayer later where we will see that for some people, thinking of God is their primary prayer expression, and that for all of us, thought is an important dimension of our being that needs to be attuned to the divine if our life is to become prayer.

[7]This memorable quote is from the inaugural address of Abraham Kuyper at the dedication of the Free University of Amsterdam: "There is not a square inch in the whole domain of our human existence over which Christ, who is Sovereign over all, does not cry: 'Mine!' " (Abraham Kuyper, "Sphere Sovereignty," in James D. Bratt, *Abraham Kuyper: A Centennial Reader* [Grand Rapids: Eerdmans, 1988], p. 488).

[8]See Richard Rohr, *The Naked Now: Learning to See as the Mystics See* (New York: Crossroad, 2009) for an excellent discussion of the presence to self and God that is associated with living nakedly in the present.

[9]The posthumous publication of sixty-six years of correspondence of Mother Teresa with her confessors and spiritual superiors (*Mother Teresa: Come Be My Light—The Private Writings of the Saint of Calcutta* [New York: Doubleday, 2007]) offers a complementary, rather than, as sometimes asserted, contradictory, perspective on the life of this remarkable woman. In this correspondence she reveals that despite a period between 1946 and 1947 when she experienced a profound sense of

union with God, soon after she began her work with the destitute and dying in Calcutta and lasting nearly a half-century until her death, she felt no presence of God whatsoever. Far from being a God-intoxicated saint who spent her days in ecstatic mystic union, she learned to deal with her protracted dark night of the soul by converting her feelings of abandonment by God into a life of abandonment to God.

[10]John O'Donohue, *Divine Beauty: The Invisible Embrace* (New York: Bantam, 2003), p. 7.

Chapter 5: Prayer as Pondering

[1]See, for example, Elaine Graham, *Theological Reflections: Methods,* vol. 1 (London: SCM Press, 2005); Robert L. Kinast, *What Are They Saying About Theological Reflection?* (New York: Paulist, 2000); or *Making Faith-Sense: Theological Reflection in Everyday Life* (Collegeville, Minn.: Liturgical Press, 1999).

[2]Nietzsche expressed a similar thought when he suggested that one should never trust a thought that did not arise from walking.

[3]Al Hsu, personal communication, November 16, 2009.

[4]I happily acknowledge my indebtedness to my wife, Juliet Benner, for this understanding not only of the importance of the imagination in prayer but also for ways we can bring imagination to our engagement with Scriptures.

[5]See, for example, Juliet Benner, *Contemplative Vision: A Guide to Christian Art and Prayer* (Downers Grove, Ill.: InterVarsity Press, forthcoming). Art based on specific biblical passages can be easily found under the "Art Index" tab on www.textweek.com.

Chapter 6: Prayer as Responding

[1]This prayer is found in two places in the Bible. Luke 11:2-4 presents a short version while Matthew 6:9-13 presents the longer version. With one exception, the long version differs from the shorter one only by being a somewhat fuller expression of thoughts that are more tersely presented in the Gospel of Luke. The more substantive difference is that Matthew includes a closing phrase ("for yours is the kingdom and the power and the glory forever and ever. Amen") that is not part of the Luke text. Roman Catholics traditionally do not include this closing phrase whereas Protestants do. Scholars (see, for example, Bruce M. Metzger, *A Textual Commentary on the Greek New Testament* [New York: United Bible Societies, 1971], pp. 16-17) suggest that it was probably not part of Jesus' original words but an adaptation of his prayer for liturgical use by the early church. The version quoted in the text is taken from The Canadian Book of Common Prayer as found at http://prayerbook.ca/bcp/holy_communion.html.

[2]This other book is titled *Soulful Spirituality: Becoming Fully Alive and Deeply Human.* It explores the way spirituality can make us either more or less deeply and authentically human by examining a number of spiritual practices that are deeply Christian even though none of them are distinctively Christian. These practices represent, therefore, foundational spiritual ways of living that support the human developmental journey.

[3]I speak of my father, Gordon Wilson Benner.

[4]For more on the role of creativity and originality in Christian spirituality, see my

book *The Gift of Being Yourself: The Sacred Call to Self-Discovery* (Downers Grove, Ill.: InterVarsity Press, 2004).

[5]The Jesus Prayer, a form of contemplative prayer that is central to Orthodox Christian spirituality, is discussed more fully in chapter seven.

[6]Passing beads through one's fingers as an aid to prayer had long been in practice before these first Christians adapted it to Christian prayer. Islam, Buddhism, Hinduism, Sikhism and Baha'ism all make use of prayer beads.

[7]The rosary begins with the Our Father (the Lord's Prayer) and then moves through the Hail Mary ("Hail Mary, full of grace, the Lord is with thee. Blessed art thou among women, and blessed is the fruit of thy womb, Jesus. Holy Mary, Mother of God, pray for us sinners now, and at the hour of death"), the Gloria Patri ("Glory be to the Father, and to the Son and to the Holy Ghost: As it was in the beginning, is now, and ever shall be, world without end. Amen"), another round of Hail Marys, and is then completed by a final praying of the Gloria Patri.

[8]Irene Alexander, "Pilgrimage: Trusting Myself to the Other," *Conversations*, fall-winter 2007, p. 45.

Chapter 7: Prayer as Being

[1]I take this analogy from James Finley, *Christian Meditation: Experiencing the Presence of God* (New York: HarperOne, 2004), who uses it to contrast meditation and contemplation.

[2]Abraham Heschel, quoted in *Man Is Not Alone: A Philosophy of Religion* (New York: Farrar, Straus & Giroux, 1976), p. 13.

[3]In contemplation we surrender our need to subject experience to analysis and reduce it to propositions. Unlike meditation, which is based on thinking and in which we try to fit whatever we encounter into our framework of understanding, in contemplation we simply stand in amazement and awe, later allowing our understanding to adjust to what we have encountered.

[4]Gerald May, *Will and Spirit* (New York: Harper & Row, 1983), p. 25.

[5]M. Basil Pennington, personal communication, October 13, 2003.

[6]This list is drawn from quotations on contemplative prayer and living presented by the Shalem Institute for Spiritual Formation <www.shalem.org/index.php/resources/quotations>.

[7]John of the Cross, *Dark Night of the Soul* (New York: Image, 1959).

[8]*The Way of a Pilgrim,* trans. H. Bacovcin (New York: Doubleday, 1985).

[9]The best introduction to the Jesus prayer is Lev Gillet, *The Jesus Prayer* (New York: St. Vladimir's Seminary Press, 1987). Simple but profound, this little book explores the theology, psychology and spiritual implications of invoking the name of Jesus, and shows how by doing so Jesus can become the integrating center of our being.

[10]The Jesus Prayer is based on prayer of the publican: "Lord, have mercy on me, a sinner," as recorded in Luke 18:10-14.

[11]Thomas Keating, *Open Mind, Open Heart: The Contemplative Dimension of the Gospel* (New York: Continuum, 2000), p. 39.

[12]Cynthia Bourgeault, *Centering Prayer and Inner Awakening* (Cambridge, Mass.: Cowley, 2004), pp. 24-25.

[13]*The Cloud of Unknowing*, trans. James Walsh (New York: HarperCollins, 1981).

[14]See Basil Pennington, *Centering Prayer: Renewing an Ancient Christian Prayer Form*

(New York: Image Books, 2001), and Thomas Keating, *Invitation to Love: The Way of Christian Contemplation* (Snowmass, Colo.: St. Benedict's Monastery, 1992).

[15]Pennington, *Centering Prayer*, p. xvi.

[16]See chapter eight of Bourgeault's *Centering Prayer* for an excellent discussion of the theology of centering prayer.

[17]Bourgeault, *Centering Prayer*, p. 6.

[18]Keating, *Invitation to Love*, p. 90.

[19]Brother Lawrence, *Cultivating the Presence of God* (Grand Rapids: Revell, 1967).

Chapter 8: Life as Prayer, Prayer as Life

[1]Etty Hillesum, *Etty Hillesum: An Interrupted Life—The Diaries, 1941-1943* (New York: Holt Paperbacks, 1996).

[2]The question might be asked how we can be certain that we are, in fact, encountering God. William Barry offers a helpful discussion of this complex issue in his *Spiritual Direction and the Encounter with God* (New York: Paulist, 1992), where he notes that "faith and experience mutually reinforce one another. If I did not believe in God, I would not experience him, although I might have to engage in some rationalizations to explain away some of my experiences. But because I believe in God I discover in my experience more than what at first blush seemed to be there and name that 'more' God. The experience reinforces my belief. . . . In other words, the believer encounters God, and knows God prior to any reflection on the experience and prior to really knowing what has been experienced. The disciples on the road to Emmaus felt their hearts burning even before they knew Jesus in the breaking of bread. When they came to believe, then they knew what they had experienced; and the reflected experience reinforced belief" (p. 31).

[3]Developed by Mary Mrozowski as way to move centering prayer from a meditative practice into active life, welcoming prayer is described in Cynthia Bourgeault, *Centering Prayer and Inner Awakening* (Cambridge, Mass.: Cowley, 2004), pp. 135-52.

[4]Chief among the supports that monastic life provides for prayer is the Liturgy of the Hours (sometimes called the Divine Office). Based on Psalm 119:164, this is built around the psalmist's habit of praising God seven times a day. In a Cistercian monastery, the Liturgy of the Hours begins with vigils (sometimes called the Night Watch) at 3:30 a.m., continuing through the day with lauds at 6 a.m., terce at 9 a.m., sext at noon, none at 3 p.m., vespers at 6 p.m., the day concluding with compline at 8 p.m. The eighteen hours of waking is thus filled with readings from Scriptures, chanting of psalms from the Psalter, and liturgical and silent prayer. Returning to silence after each of these services then builds in the rhythm of silence and the Word that I described in chapter three as the ideal way to ground prayer in the rhythm of life. With slight modifications of time, content and exact number of offices, this pattern of daily prayer is encouraged for all monks, nuns and priests in the Roman Catholic Church, as well as the Anglican Church and the Eastern Orthodox Church. Many lay Christians also adopt the Divine Office—in part or in whole—as the backbone of their own daily prayer.

Chapter 9: Transformational Prayer

[1]Thomas Keating, *Open Heart, Open Mind* (New York: Continuum, 2000), p. 4.

[2]Evagrius Ponticus, quoted in Kallistos Ware, *The Philokalia*, trans. G. E. H. Palmer,

Philip Sherrard and Kallistos Ware (London: Faber & Faber, 1984), 3:96.

[3]Anthony of the Desert, quoted in Keating, *Open Heart, Open Mind*, p. 91.

[4]The phrase "the unloading of the unconscious" comes from Thomas Keating (*Open Heart, Open Mind*), who, along with Cynthia Bourgeault (*Centering Prayer and Inner Awakening* [Cambridge, Mass.: Cowley, 2004]) offers us one of the most helpful accounts and understandings of this process of divine therapy.

[5]I tell this man's story with his permission, but at his request I will keep his identity confidential. The same is true of the case of "Tom" presented later in this chapter.

formatio

TRADITION. EXPERIENCE.
TRANSFORMATION.

Formatio books from InterVarsity Press follow the rich tradition of the church in the journey of spiritual formation. These books are not merely about being informed, but about being transformed by Christ and conformed to his image. Formatio stands in InterVarsity Press's evangelical publishing tradition by integrating God's Word with spiritual practice and by prompting readers to move from inward change to outward witness. InterVarsity Press uses the chambered nautilus for Formatio, a symbol of spiritual formation because of its continual spiral journey outward as it moves from its center. We believe that each of us is made with a deep desire to be in God's presence. Formatio books help us to fulfill our deepest desires and to become our true selves in light of God's grace.